Just Good Teaching

Comprehensive Musicianship through Performance (CMP) in Theory and Practice

Laura K. Sindberg

Published in partnership with
NAFME: National Association for Music Education

ROWMAN & LITTLEFIELD EDUCATION

A division of
ROWMAN & LITTLEFIELD PUBLISHERS, INC.
Lanham • New York • Toronto • Plymouth, UK

Published in partnership with NAFME: National Association for Music Education

Published by Rowman & Littlefield Education
A division of Rowman & Littlefield Publishers, Inc.
A wholly owned subsidary of The Rowman & Littlefield Publishing Group, Inc.
4501 Forbes Boulevard, Suite 200, Lanham, Maryland 20706
www.rowman.com

10 Thornbury Road, Plymouth PL6 7PP, United Kingdom

British Library Cataloguing in Publication Information Available

Library of Congress Cataloging-in-Publication Data

Sindberg, Laura.
  Just good teaching : comprehensive musicianship through performance (CMP) in theory and practice / Laura Sindberg.
    p. cm.
  "Published in partnership with NAFME: The National Association for Music Education."
  Includes bibliographical references and index.
  ISBN 978-1-61048-339-1 (cloth : alk. paper)—ISBN 978-1-61048-340-7 (pbk. : alk. paper)— ISBN 978-1-61048-341-4 (electronic)
  1. Music—Instruction and study. I. National Association for Music Education. II. Title.
  MT1.S532 2011
  780.71—dc23
                                                                                2011048067

Dedicated to the students.
After all, it's all because of you.

Contents

Figures and Tables

LIST OF FIGURES

LIST OF TABLES

Foreword

The main title of this book, *Just Good Teaching*, invites reflection on the nature of music teachers' work. Good music teachers are like architects. They seek out the best raw materials (sound) incorporated into beautifully crafted designs and forms (musical works). Within a work, they highlight these intersecting relationships of sound so that the artistry of the design can be apprehended and appreciated by others. Each carefully chosen work contributes to the realization of the overall master plan (the repertoire as curriculum), which is constructed to enhance students' experiences with a variety of meaningful musical examples.

Good music teachers are also like choreographers sensitive to the shifting movement and energy of human interactions. They plan instruction so that students are engaged in patterns of music making and taking that ebb and flow. They pay attention to who leads the classroom "dance" as well as who follows, and often mix up familiar patterns so that students' participation is more satisfying, compelling, and arrestingly unpredictable. Through these choreographic moves, a group of disparate individuals comes together to function as an ensemble.

Good music teachers resemble naturalists as well, looking for subtle patterns and variations in students' musical understanding and awareness. They probe beyond the commonplace to uncover how students think about and respond to music. They make note of individual differences while working with an entire roomful of developing musicians at once. Mindful of these important distinctions, they continually adjust their teaching to respond to students' work in flexible and interactive ways.

These are but a few of the roles that good music teachers embrace as they undertake the worthy aim of providing a quality music education for students (others might include a detective who collects evidence of learning, an air traffic controller who organizes complex sequences of events, or a judge who arbitrates conflicting opinions and interpretations). You might enjoy adding to this playful mix of similes and roles to characterize the breadth and depth required of individuals we acknowledge and set apart as *good music teachers*.

The view of comprehensive musicianship forwarded in this book is a distillation of the wisdom of practice exhibited by such thoughtful and forward-thinking music teachers. Laura Sindberg, who exemplifies these admirable attributes herself, has provided an historical, theoretical, conceptual, and practical overview of Comprehensive Musicianship through Performance (CMP), which will be illuminating for preservice and inservice music educators, as well as music teacher educators, interested in broadening their visions of the music curriculum.

Performance is the hallmark of ensembles. School bands, orchestras, and choirs have remained the primary avenue for music teaching and learning in secondary schools throughout much of the twentieth and early twenty-first century (although other curricular offerings for middle and high school are showing promising signs of expansion). During public performances, audience members are often impressed by the precision and expressivity of a school ensemble's musical offerings. Through sequentially organized programs of instruction and considerable practice and refinement, young musicians attain remarkably high standards of performance. Music educators, whose expertise facilitates this growth, are understandably proud of these accomplishments. At the same time, many have raised the paradoxical reality that high-quality ensemble performance is highly dependent upon the musical abilities of individual students, but sometimes the instructional practices of the ensemble—where the focus is primarily on the group—stand in the way of individual growth and independence. This is the central argument for adopting a more comprehensive view of music teaching and learning in an ensemble setting.

Comprehensive, in this sense, challenges us to move toward a more capacious stance—"more is more" (in contrast to Mies van der Rohe's famous dictum, "less is more"). CMP embraces and fosters high levels of performance achievement while also challenging the perceptual acuity of students through greater emphases on listening, evaluating, shaping, and interpreting works. It also aims to develop students' integrated historical and contextual knowledge about music. Teaching music "with its roots on" often implicates performance practice. In addition, students are encouraged to consider the composer's craft, aware of the compositional devices and decisions that bring artistry to the forefront of understanding.

As Sindberg so cogently illustrates through quotes, anecdotes, teaching plans, and musical examples, music teachers committed to comprehensive programs put these beliefs into action as they approach curriculum, instruction, and assessment. Repertoire, which stands as the organizing center of CMP, serves as the springboard for analysis, outcomes, strategies, and assessments. Well-chosen choral and instrumental works are the vehicles through which musical exploration occurs.

One of the most precious commodities in education is instructional time; teacher-conductors of ensembles often strive for efficient and highly structured rehearsals. Accordingly, the balance of decision making tips toward the conductor, who oversees the use of every valuable minute to prepare for public performance. Rehearsals that run like clockwork, where not a minute is wasted, are sought after. However, when efficiency is weighed against the breadth of aims suggested by comprehensive musicianship, instructional priorities shift. The path toward student engagement is often more circuitous, indirect, and time consuming, but when the benefits of sharing responsibility for musical decisions and interpretation arise, the educational impact is convincing. Throughout this book, there are numerous examples of creative strategies that offer compelling accounts of students' musical understanding that complements, rather than competes with, expressive performance.

Ensemble rehearsals are primary examples of formative assessment at its finest as conductors and performers translate gesture and critique into immediate changes in sound. Assessing individual growth is more challenging, however, particularly with the large enrollment typical of ensembles. CMP also speaks to innovative forms of assessment, as teachers design activities to gather rich evidence of students' cognitive, skill-based, and affective development.

In any field, conceptions of good teaching practice will vary; this variance is a sign of health. The profession depends upon clearly articulated models, pedagogical systems, and engaging methods for teachers to consider, investigate, adopt, and modify. For music educators who seek a well-integrated, adaptable, and musically sound approach to cultivating students' musical independence in choral and instrumental ensembles, this book will be of great interest. Sindberg's descriptions of her own practice as well as portraits of music teachers in the field and their applications of the CMP model testify to its flexible use and widespread value. *Just Good Teaching: Comprehensive Musicianship through Performance (CMP) in Theory and Practice* furnishes us with inspiring possibilities for meaningful and engaging music learning and teaching.

Janet R. Barrett
chair, Society for
Music Teacher Education;
associate professor,
Northwestern University

Preface

Teachers in school music ensembles (band, choir, orchestra) plan instruction that will lead to student learning—learning most often focused on technical skill development. Such are the traditions of the performance ensemble. The value of teaching students beyond technical proficiencies toward a broader body of knowledge and understanding has been supported by many authors, but its acceptance is less clear.

A model exists that is designed to lead to a broader musical experience in the ensemble setting. Comprehensive Musicianship through Performance (CMP) is a framework for planning instruction that promotes a holistic form of music learning. It is a planned process to guide instruction in cognitive, affective, and skill development. Or, in the words of a good friend, "know, do, and feel." The CMP model consists of five planning points: analysis, assessment, music selection, outcomes, and strategies. When applied to a musical composition, the result is a teaching plan that invites students to fully engage with the music as they perform, listen to, describe, analyze, compare, and explore the compositions in their band folders. Or choir folders. Or orchestra folders.

I was exposed to CMP as a novice teacher . . . well, that is not entirely true. As an undergraduate music ed student I did have an assignment that had something to do with CMP. At the time, it was just another assignment, completed and forgotten. It was years later, when I was starting out as a teacher, that I encountered CMP as a significant influence. Instantly engaging and deeply challenging, it provided structure and organization to ideas I had about teaching music. I wanted my class to be a setting in which we tried out ideas. I wanted my students to be as excited about and interested in music as I was. I did not want to be bored and I did not want my students to be bored. CMP fed into my emerging philosophy. From the event of my first workshop I embraced this model, passionate to bring a meaningful experience to my students; to encourage their curiosity about music. My commitment to CMP was not always met with favor by students, parents, and colleagues, as it strayed from what they were accustomed to. This was challenging. But I had found a support system in the CMP steering committee, and this was instrumental in enacting the vision I had for my students. Over time I saw what I believed to be a more holistic awareness of music on the part of the students. As parents began to understand the reasons why students were writing, discussing, composing, and evaluating music, they also responded positively to the comprehensive experience their children were having.

I wrote this book because as teacher-conductors,[1] we have an opportunity to reinvigorate the rehearsal room. One of the ways this can happen is by getting students more engaged in their experience by providing rich and varied opportunities in addition to "playing." The CMP model is a useful approach to broadening and deepening the musical experience in the ensemble setting and allows teachers, at the same time, to exercise their own particular beliefs and creativity. It is a framework for planning instruction, not a prescription for how to teach. CMP depends on the teacher's knowledge of his or her subject, students, and pedagogy as the framework is fleshed out into a teaching plan. This model originated from best practices in the classroom, informed by similar efforts to bring about a more comprehensive musical experience for students. It continues through the efforts of teachers who serve on the CMP Project in Wisconsin and also in an increasing number of states as well as teacher education programs. This book tells the story of CMP, from classrooms where teachers apply the model for planning instruction in their band, choir, and orchestra rooms. It is for teachers (including teacher educators) who have in mind a musical experience for their students that has deep roots and broad branches.

The purpose of this book is to describe CMP in terms of its theoretical foundations and practical application in the ensemble setting (band, choir, orchestra). CMP was introduced in 1977 during an era of school reform in the United

States and has continued for over thirty years. *Just Good Teaching: Comprehensive Musicianship through Performance (CMP) in Theory and Practice* includes a description of the evolution of CMP and its connections to other forms of comprehensive musicianship that emerged during a period of educational reform in the post-Sputnik era. A detailed description of the CMP model provides the foundation for a discussion of planning and implementation as the model is enacted in the ensemble setting. The discrete planning points of the CMP model are considered in relation to a broader context. Several musical examples help illuminate this material. This book is not the authoritative text on comprehensive musicianship. It chronicles CMP, one approach that shares several of the goals of other such efforts under the "comprehensive musicianship umbrella" (Mitchell, 1969, p. 71).

One of the key components of this book is the inclusion of anecdotes. These anecdotes come from classrooms in which CMP is practiced, including my own. I visited many classrooms and talked with many teacher-conductors. The anecdotes are included for two reasons: First, to personalize the material, which may otherwise seem tedious, while simultaneously giving voice to the teacher-conductor working to incorporate this framework; second, to demonstrate how principles of CMP can be incorporated into the band, choir, and orchestra room without compromising the integrity of the program (one may even question the integrity of a rehearsal that does not include an emphasis on CMP as less-than-best-quality . . . but we leave this to the reader to consider).

The notion of pairing theory and practice under one cover may surprise some readers. There is a tendency among published volumes to be directed toward practitioners *or* scholars. In my view, there is room for both. In this book I have sought to address CMP in a manner that speaks to practicing teachers. For example, by applying the CMP model to two arrangements of the same folk song, "Shenandoah," we can see the fluidity of the CMP model. The inclusion of a chapter describing the origins of the CMP model has relevance for graduate students and teacher educators who wish to study the historical context of CMP; this context is also relevant for teachers, many of whom make ongoing learning a part of their work.

NOTE

1. The term, teacher-conductor, may be unfamiliar to some readers; however, it speaks to the dual roles assumed by those working with students in large ensembles.

Acknowledgments

I have been the beneficiary of countless excellent teachers, of music and other subjects, in school and out of school, all of whom I cannot possibly name here. But it pretty much began with Mr. Yindra. A crusty band director, he laid out high expectations we would not *think* of questioning. He taught us that we made band what it was, that it was special because of us. We didn't necessarily know that we were exceptional, but he showed us that we could be. There was my saxophone teacher, Mrs. Orlaska, another taskmaster who practiced the art of "tough love." Mr. Kirchhoff followed Mr. Yindra, maintaining standards of excellence with youthful exuberance. You were all so incredibly committed to music and to your students—and we were so very fortunate.

In my undergraduate education, Will Schmid, Gerry McKenna, and John Downey stand out for their wisdom, intelligence, humanity, and good humor. I thank each of these teachers for the gifts they have shared, explicit lessons of content and implicit lessons of good teaching. I acknowledge the generous support of members of the CMP Project, fellow teachers who are relentless in their pursuit of musical understanding through performance in their own practice as well as through countless inservice and workshop sessions. For over twenty years I have had the honor of working among you and learning from you.

I thank my teaching colleagues in the public schools. Since my first teaching days at Roosevelt Middle School of the Arts there have been too many of you to name, but you have been role models for me as well as our students. Working in community with you has been a privilege for which I am endlessly grateful.

Thanks to my friends and colleagues who lent assistance from the very beginning, critiquing proposals, reading chapters, and sharing ideas and encouragement. Thanks to the many teachers and students who contributed anecdotes, especially Miriam Altman, Susan McAllister, and Gary Wolfman. Colin Holter engraved musical excerpts with a keen eye, patiently revising as needed for best-quality musical examples. Thanks to Mr. Gabriel and his students, who allowed me to watch as the study of *Battalia* unfolded. Gratitudes to the wise teachers who came before me and to the countless students in my life, always challenging me to be a better teacher. Most of all, I thank my husband and partner, Gary, who read, reread, and questioned each chapter multiple times, always with an open and kind heart.

1

Looking in a CMP Classroom

. . . and also, you know, he dedicated his piece to a god of wine, which was interesting. I didn't realize that it was so incredibly satirical until we delved into that aspect . . . the "Battle" . . . it didn't seem like a serious battle . . . then after I realized that we also delved deeper into the second movement ("The Profligate Society of Common Humor") . . . and I started to realize how we were all starting to feel lost while we were playing different tunes. At first I was confused about why we were doing this. It sounded so . . . it sounded really bad at first. Mr. Gabriel helped us to see the deepness of how far it (the music) went.

—high school orchestra student, Linden High School[1]

CLASS BEGINS

Where does good teaching begin? With the teacher? The students? What *is* good music teaching? An Internet search revealed a myriad of resources, from lists of teacher personality traits to demonstration videos to articles and online discussions, all of which provide answers to these questions. Most likely, there is no clear starting point—good teaching might begin any number of ways. Schmidt (1998) sought to address the question by examining beliefs of student teachers and found their definitions to be idiosyncratic and context specific, particular to individuals. Lehman (1986) highlights the difficulties in attempting to define good music teaching and says that it goes beyond lists of skills, knowledge, and personality traits. When we think about our own experiences as teachers and as students, Schmidt and Lehman's descriptions resonate. While we may not be able to answer the question of where good teaching begins or what exactly it is, there is merit in asking. Here, we begin in the classroom.

This chapter includes selected vignettes from the Linden High School orchestra room in which students rehearsed *Battalia* (ed. Blahnik, 1999), by Heinrich Ignaz Franz Biber (1644–1704).[2] The vignettes were selected from among several rehearsals that were videotaped and transcribed during the weeks this piece was being prepared for performance. Each "day" describes learning activities created by Mr. Gabriel for his students—snapshots of the rehearsal. Mr. Gabriel is a veteran teacher with more than thirty-five years of teaching experience at Linden High School in Lakeview. Linden High School is one of three public high schools in Lakeview, a city of approximately 70,000 in the Midwest. *Battalia* is one of several compositions that the orchestra is rehearsing as they prepare for their first concert of the year. It is multimovement work, arranged for strings by Joel Blahnik (1999). Score excerpts are included in the appendix. The titles of the movements are as follows:

1. "Sonata"
2. "The Profligate Society of Common Humor"
3. "Allegro"
4. "The March"
5. "Presto"
6. "Aria"
7. "The Battle"
8. "The Lament of the Wounded"

DAY ONE—INTRODUCING *BATTALIA*

The bell has rung and students are engaged in their warm-up routine, one student on the podium leading the warm-ups, which includes selection of a scale, various bowings, articulations, and rhythms. Mr. Gabriel then steps on the podium and asks students to play scales in multiple keys simultaneously: first violins F major, second violins A major, violas G major, cellos and basses C major. Following this unusual exercise, he asks, "What did that sound like? How many of you liked that sound? How many of you didn't like that sound?" Students comment informally, some laugh at what seems to be a weird or silly sound. Their teacher asks students to take out the piece that they think has dissonance. Several pull *Battalia* from their folders; another bunch selects an arrangement of "Paint It Black." Mr. Gabriel embraces the teaching moment, asking students why they chose the piece they did, and redirects everyone to *Battalia*. The orchestra then reads through the second movement of *Battalia*—"The Profligate Society of Common Humor".[3] Mr. Gabriel and the students follow the reading with a discussion about what might be happening in the music; he asks several questions and introduces two musical terms: polytonality and polyrhythms.

Next, Mr. Gabriel invites the students to "create a unique sound that you can make on your instrument." They are told to work in pairs or small groups. Students quickly busy themselves with this intriguing task. After a few minutes, the musicians share examples of the sounds they created, an interesting display of ingenuity. "Look through *Battalia* and find the places where you have different sounds." Students flip through their parts in search of unconventional sounds notated in their parts. Their teacher talks them through the first several movements of *Battalia*. Together, teacher and students analyze their music in a search for "different sounds." Movement 1—the unusual sounds of striking the instrument with the wood of the bow; movement 2—no unusual sounds; movement 3—no unusual sounds; movement 4—"Basses, what do you have?" The basses put a piece of paper between the strings and draw the bow across. "What does that sound like?" "Like a snare drum," one student volunteers. "Are there other unique sounds used in this piece? What are they and where are they?"

Mr. Gabriel asks the students about Biber: "When did he live? During what musical period?" Students look at his dates listed on their parts, then refer to a giant timeline of composers painted on one side of the orchestra room and see that Biber lived and worked during the Baroque era. Mr. Gabriel talks to the students about the advanced techniques Biber used, and says that they were very unusual techniques, particularly during the Baroque era.

DAY TWO—SOUNDS DIFFERENT

Today's rehearsal of *Battalia* begins with a question from the teacher. "What do you think this piece is about?" He looks around the room, patiently waiting while students consider the question. Several students respond: "each movement has a certain kind of emotion"; "the piece is about a battle"; "each movement describes an emotion related to battle." The questioning continues as the discussion moves to a deeper level, concerned with emotional and descriptive aspects of the work.

Teacher: If that is true, what kind of emotion would the first movement describe?

Students: Excitement, anticipation, joy.

The group plays the first two movements of *Battalia*, "Sonata" and "The Profligate Society of Common Humor." Their teacher asks, "Which movement do you think describes a party?"

The students are unsure. Their teacher asks that they play the movements again and provides a focus: "As we play movements 1 and 2, I want you to tell me what the emotion might be, or what part of the battle might be depicted." After playing the first movement several students suggest that this movement describes a gathering of troops or soldiers marching. Mr. Gabriel reminds students that in the Baroque era wealthy people would hire mercenaries to fight battles.

Teacher: Do they [the soldiers] all come from the same place?

Students: No.

Teacher: How does the music portray that they are coming from different places?

Students: Dynamics, some coming from near, some from far, different people, different sounds.

Teacher: What else in the music tells us that the people are not coming from the same place?

Students: Polytonality. (several students respond)

As the students play they are asked to figure out why Biber used polytonality. After they finish playing the movement, the students speculate that perhaps individual groups of troops are at their own camps. Mr. Gabriel instructs each part (violin 1, 2, 3, viola, etc.) to position themselves around the room, to replicate their own "camp." Each part or section is asked to come up with a name for their group, select a simple song ("Twinkle, Twinkle, Little Star"; "Row, Row, Row Your Boat"; etc.) and sing it.

After a few minutes of organizing and rehearsing, the students perform their songs at the same time. As one might imagine, the result is loud, chaotic, and celebratory. Students return to their original seats and play the movement again. Mr. Gabriel reminds them of the contextual aspects of this piece and says, "Biber was very much ahead of his time."

DAY THREE—GOING DEEPER

"Today's work centers on digging deeper into what some of the movements of *Battalia* are about." Mr. Gabriel sets out his intentions and the work begins. In relation to the second movement ("The Profligate Society of Common Humor") Mr. Gabriel asks, "What is this movement about?"

Student: Groups of soldiers sitting around a fire, singing their own songs.

Teacher: And how does the composer make that happen?

Student: Polytonality.

Teacher: And what is that?

Student: Using different keys.

They are also asked about some of the meters Biber uses in this movement; selected sections are asked to play their parts. The cellos play for the group and students identify the meter as 4/4. When the violins play, their meter is identified as 6/8. Their teacher asks them to speculate on the meaning of *profligate* and share their ideas with their stand partners. Mr. Gabriel then shares a definition that a student left anonymously on his desk: *recklessly, with a sense of humor.* "Let's play the movement recklessly, with a sense of humor." Technical details are not ignored, and Mr. Gabriel reminds students, "If this movement portrays a group moving, the repeated eighth notes should get louder." Again, their imaginations are engaged in their personal interpretation and performance of the second movement (see appendix A).

Next, the group reads the third movement ("Allegro") and are faced with more questions: "Does the composer give any idea of what this movement is about? What do you think this movement is about?" The group plays it again, but are given a prompt: "Try to think of what mood this is trying to get across." Students begin to speculate as their teacher has asked, and a lengthy discussion follows. Together, they work to discover what Biber was trying to express as well as the tools he used in his work.

Teacher: Do you think the groups are feeling some joy and some doubt as they gather together?

Student: Maybe they are uneasy and uncertain about what is going to happen.

Teacher: How does the composer create doubt or uneasiness while at the same time joy?

Student: Changes in dynamics . . .

Maybe the last chord . . .

Teacher: What do you mean?

Student: It sounds unfinished . . .

The dotted rhythm might show some hesitation . . .

Or people trying to talk to each other, like a dialogue . . .

Teacher: How many measures are there in this movement?

Student: Seven.

Teacher: Is seven a normal length for a musical phrase?

Student: No.

Again, the questions invite imagination, speculation. One student uses his violin to express the idea of a repeated motive and demonstrates, through playing, how this movement has no ending and just continues from one voice to another. In fact, the entire movement is just seven measures (see appendix A).

Teacher: All of your answers are very interesting. Let's play the movement again and see if you have a different feeling for it. See if you can get that feeling of joy and doubt at the same time.

After the group plays the movement again, they review the piece and consider the various emotions that have been realized in the first three movements. A few corrections are made about bowing and counting; at one point the cellos are asked to listen to the second violins and identify the note that was played out of tune. And the rehearsal continues.

DAY FOUR—A LETTER HOME

The discussion of Biber's motives continues with movements 2, 7, and 6. "Aria," movement 6, has not yet been read by the group. After playing movements 2 and 7 and briefly discussing what Biber might be trying to depict, the teacher guides the orchestra to a reading of movement 6.

Teacher: Today I would like to do the movement we haven't done yet. Which movement is that?

Student: "Aria."

"Let's sight read that." The orchestra reads through "Aria." "Go back to the beginning. Play *piano.*" After the group plays through "Aria" at the appropriate dynamic marking, Mr. Gabriel asks them to take out their portfolios. "Don't talk. I want you to answer two questions: What emotion or action of battle is Biber trying to depict in this movement? Why is this piece called 'Aria?'"
The students write for several minutes and are then asked to share their responses:

Student: Calm before the storm, preparation . . .

> After they say goodbye to everyone and are sad—they don't know if they will see their family again.

> They are afraid of battle . . .

> Worried about going into battle . . .

> Calm before the storm—they know the battle is going to come.

> The song expresses the idea of a prayer.

Many students share their thoughts. The feeling in the room is intimate, despite the presence of seventy string players. When their teacher asks why the movement is called "Aria," he also mentions the musical definition of aria as a musical composition sung by a solo singer. One student says that she thinks the movement is called "Aria" because the soldiers are feeling alone.

Teacher: What I'd like you to do is . . . I want you to imagine you are being shipped off to Iraq or Afghanistan. And you are writing a letter to your family, not knowing whether or not you will come back. Write a letter to your family. We won't be sharing these.

Students spend several minutes composing their letters. The room is dead quiet, with an intense silence. Students are deeply immersed in their own thoughts. When their teacher notices that many students are done with their letters, he tells them there will be two more minutes of writing time; they should finish their thoughts. After two minutes, Mr. Gabriel asks students to stop, even if they are not done writing, and announces that they will play the "Aria." He speaks in a very soft tone so as not to disturb the environment that had been created when students were writing their letters. Following their performance of this movement, there are several seconds of silence. Rehearsal continues as the orchestra continues to the next movement ("The Battle").

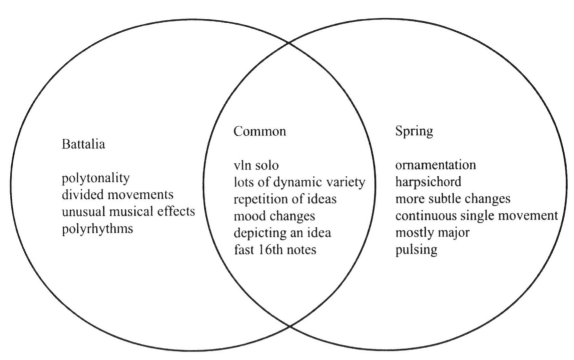

Figure 1.1. Venn Diagram

The circles contain the following text:

Battalia

polytonality
divided movements
unusual musical effects
polyrhythms

Common

vln solo
lots of dynamic variety
repetition of ideas
mood changes
depicting an idea
fast 16th notes

Spring

ornamentation
harpsichord
more subtle changes
continuous single movement
mostly major
pulsing

DAY FIVE—BIBER AND THE BAROQUE

Teacher: As you see, the sheet I passed out to you contains a Venn diagram. I am going to play for you another piece from the Baroque era. The composer is Antonio Vivaldi, and the piece is called *Spring.* It is one of the movements of the *Four Seasons,* a very famous piece. What I want you to do is label one circle *Spring* and the other *Battalia.* The outer sections of the circle are for things that are unique to each piece. Where the circles intersect, list things you hear that are in both pieces. Both pieces are from the Baroque era.

The orchestra listens to the recording and completes the Venn diagram. Mr. Gabriel asks for a student volunteer to write responses on the board.

After responses are listed, a brief discussion of the differences and similarities between the two pieces follows. "Put the Venn diagram in your portfolio and put *Battalia* away." The rehearsal continues with other repertoire that the ensemble is rehearsing (there is a concert approaching, after all).

DAY SIX—*BATTALIA* AS SATIRE?

Today the orchestra begins with the first movement of *Battalia.* Technical corrections are made in several areas as the group plays through the movement. Mr. Gabriel asks his students, "If you were a listener, what would you think when you heard the first movement? What might draw your attention?" Teacher and students proceed to examine each movement of *Battalia*; the musical detectives speculate on the devices Biber uses to portray or describe aspects of war. After looking at the final movement ("The Lament of the Wounded"), the investigation moves to another level when Mr. Gabriel asks students to discuss with their stand partner whether or not *Battalia* is a satire. They review the definition of satire, sharing examples from other contexts. Their teacher asks, "Is this piece a satire, or is Biber just showing the different emotions of war?" After several minutes of lively discussion, responses are shared and listed on the board for all to see: "It's obnoxious—how can it be taken seriously; the movements are really short—a more serious piece would have longer movements; it's overdone, cliché."

As he often does, Mr. Gabriel probes deeper and tells the students they are missing something, to look in the music for something that might indicate *Battalia* is a satire. One student volunteers, "It's dedicated to Bacchus, the god of frivolity." A second student offers, "Biber could have dedicated the piece to a war god, but instead he dedicated it to the god of wine." Many students participate in the discussion. There appears to be a general agreement that the piece could be both serious and satirical.

Mr. Gabriel asks students to take out their portfolios, and prepare to take notes. The subject is the Thirty Years' War. There is a sharing of facts related to this particular war, who Biber was, and how the war may have influenced or affected him. Mr. Gabriel shares his point of view, telling the students that he believed Biber wrote *Battalia* to portray how ridiculous war was. "To me, this is an anti-war piece." Next, to bring the focus back to music making, he asks the students to play the "The Battle" and "The Lament of the Wounded." Always the interrogator, he asks students, "What might the three notes that are repeated at the end of the Lament represent?" The students suggest it may represent the dragging of a wounded leg or maybe the trinity of the church. Mr. Gabriel's focus consistently emphasizes an intent on the part of the students to figure out why Biber wrote the piece as he did. The orchestra continues their work on *Battalia* and other repertoire as they prepare for their first concert of the school year, diligently attending to technical details as they continue their exploration of Biber's work.

REFLECTING ON THE REHEARSAL VIGNETTES

What can we learn from these glimpses into the Linden High School orchestra room? What do the various learning activities tell us about the teacher? The students? How do the students feel about this kind of experience in their orchestra? Three themes emerge from the vignettes:

Theme #1—An intention on the part of the teacher that emphasizes use of questions to engage students and get them to think on a broader and deeper level;

Theme #2—Value of individual or personal opinion in relation to the students' interpretation of music and the composer's intent;

Theme #3—Making connections beyond the particular piece, in this case historical connections as well as connections to other Baroque works.

It is clear that Mr. Gabriel has a vision of music teaching and learning that is both deep and far-reaching. His persistent questioning, particularly in relation to what Biber is trying to portray and the ways in which he uses music to do this, are threads woven into each vignette. Early on in the study of *Battalia*, this teacher-conductor reminds students that the main question is to figure out "why Biber wrote the piece the way he did." The emphasis on why invites students to think at a deeper level and engage their imaginations as they speculate on Biber's choices. At the same time, we see evidence of error detection, correction, and attention to detail that demonstrate a value of a high level of musical performance. With the letter-writing episode, we see a particularly compelling example illustrating the affective dimension of the musical experience.

We also see a consistent effort to invite students to speculate on what they think the composer was trying to say or accomplish in this piece. Questions such as "what do you think this is about?, why do you think Biber did this?, how did he do that?," are examples of the teacher's intention to have students explore and describe how music can depict the many emotions of war. We recall the letter-writing episode of Day Four, during which students imagined they were being sent to war. One of the students shared her letter:

Dear Dad,

I'm going off to Iraq tomorrow. I want you to know that I thank you so much for all you've done for me. You took me in when my life wasn't too great with mom. You always were quite perceptive. I wish you Merry Christmas to all the upcoming Christmases that we won't share together, and sweet dreams to all the nights we won't say goodnight. I'll miss you terribly. If I don't make it home, I want you to know that my collection of books is for you. I don't want to make this letter too sappy, otherwise I'll never have the heart to send it. But you deserve the best, Dad. The absolute best for all you've done for me.

Your daughter,

There is a common thread in the vignettes, including a consistent attention to details of performance and excellence in performance as well as understandings about the selected repertoire. Correcting rhythms, notes, bowing, helping students develop sight-reading skills—this all points to a value not only of deeper musical understanding but of excellent musical performance as well. It's not just about the practice of asking students a myriad of questions; equally important is the classroom atmosphere that embraces the point of view of each student in the ensemble.

OVERVIEW OF THE BOOK

In this chapter, we took a peek into a high school string orchestra in which students participated in many varied activities. We saw that the teacher's intentions included not only a high level of performance, but facilitating learning *about* music—in this case through *Battalia* as a focus piece. This teacher's practice was comprehensive, centered on performing with understanding. Comprehensive Musicianship through Performance (CMP) is the particular framework used by this teacher in organizing instruction; it is also the focus of this book. CMP is a framework for planning instruction in school ensembles that promotes a holistic form of music learning; a planned process to guide instruction in cognitive, affective, and skill development for students in band, choir, and orchestra.

A detailed description of the CMP model provides the foundation for a discussion of planning and implementation as the model is enacted in the ensemble setting in the remaining chapters of this book. The discrete planning points of the CMP model (analysis, assessment, music selection, outcomes, and strategies) are considered in relation to a broader theoretical context, accompanied by several musical examples to help illustrate this framework. Interviews and anecdotes are included as a contextual narrative piece to personalize the material throughout the book. Samples of teaching plans, constructed by different teachers, are included in the appendixes as a resource to demonstrate how the framework can be adapted by the individual teacher to suit the needs of his or her students. Discussion questions are posed at the conclusion of each chapter to promote additional discussion.

GOING FURTHER—QUESTIONS FOR DISCUSSION

1. How might you characterize the atmosphere of this orchestra room, after reading the vignettes?
2. How does the exploration of "why a composer wrote the piece" add value to a final (in concert) performance?
3. In what ways does the teacher's use of questioning stimulate interest on the part of the students?
4. If you were a student visiting this orchestra in rehearsal, would this resemble your own experience? Describe.
5. What additional learning activities would you add to those described in these vignettes?

NOTES

1. All names and locations are pseudonyms.
2. The complete teaching plan for *Battalia* is included in the appendix.
3. This title will pique anyone's curiosity. But the reader will need to be patient . . . see Day Three.

2

The CMP Model

Performing group participation has little effect on musical behavior other than the acquisition of performance skills, unless there is a planned effort by the teacher to enrich the performing experience with additional kinds of musical understanding. (Benner, 1972, p. 10)

INTRODUCTION

The Comprehensive Musicianship through Performance (CMP) model is a framework from which teachers of performing groups (primarily band, choir, and orchestra) plan instruction. The model consists of five components, most commonly referred to as "points of the model." The five points of the model include music selection, analysis, outcomes, strategies, and assessment. Figure 2.1 depicts the various organizational components of the CMP model:

Figure 2.1. CMP Model

This chapter describes the CMP planning model in detail. Included is a thorough description of each of the planning points along with a wider perspective within music teaching and learning. We will begin with music selection, followed by analysis, outcomes, strategies, and assessment, and return to music selection. In this chapter we will refer to "The Stars and Stripes Forever" (Sousa, 1897), to inform our examination of the discrete points of the CMP model and take a close look at each one. The CMP workshop planning sheets, used to construct the teaching plan, are included in appendix B.

MUSIC SELECTION

When we, as teacher-conductors and teacher educators, select music for instruction, what causes one piece to rise to the top of the pile of collected scores? Is it the newest piece, hot off the press? Is it a tried-and-true work selected because it is familiar? Is it something recommended by a trusted colleague? What do we look at as we consider repertoire for the ensemble or for the methods student? Comprehensive musicianship calls for a detailed consideration of repertoire selection, which has also been articulated by Labuta (1997): "The music presents the problems, the solutions develop musicianship" (p. 14).

The notion that the key to good teaching is working with quality literature has been described by several authors (Hylton, 1995; Labuta, 1997; O'Toole, 2003; Reynolds, 2000). Selection of repertoire is among the most important choices a teacher-conductor makes. More than just selecting pieces for a performance, repertoire is the foundation of the curriculum in the ensemble setting (Garofalo, 1983; Labuta, 1997; Reynolds, 2000). Each of these authors calls for careful evaluation of music to determine its merit for the ensemble. Supplemental collections of techniques, chorales, and sight singing support the development of skills and knowledge that lead to high levels of performance of the selected repertoire, but it is the repertoire that forms the core of the curriculum in band, choir, and orchestra programs.

In addition, teacher-conductors often work with groups of students over multiple years—whether middle school configuration of grades 6 through 8, high school configuration of 9 through 12, or some variation thereof. The opportunity to work with students for several years places greater responsibility on the teacher to select repertoire with particular intentions. The broader implications of repertoire selection are addressed later, in chapter 6, where we discuss CMP and the music curriculum. For now, we will focus on specific considerations for selecting music.

What are the criteria for the selection of repertoire, and how do others address and promote the use of quality music? Viewed through the lens of CMP, music selected for study should be quality literature that is well crafted and beautiful; it should facilitate the learning of concepts such as musical elements, style, and technique. Labuta suggests music be "chosen for its musical worth, stylistic validity, teaching potential, and suitability for programming" (1997, p. 14). Among the primary criteria provided by Garofalo are structural elements (a high degree of compositional design, for example), historical context (representing diverse styles, historical periods, and cultures), and skills development (1983). The selection of quality repertoire is particularly critical in achieving comprehensive musicianship, according to Garofalo.

And so what is meant by "quality music," and how does one assess the quality of a composition? The CMP framework offers several questions that help guide one through the process of evaluating and selecting musical works for school ensembles. And while words such as "good" and "quality" can be intimidating at first, we must press on and not be afraid of those characteristics to take a stand in evaluating music for our students. Examples of questions included in the CMP framework are several that can help determine the quality of a composition:

- Is the piece unique?
- Does it contain a balance of predictability and surprise?
- To what extent does the composition contain depth?
- Is it well designed in relation to form?
- Is the text meaningful?

Next, we move on to questions more pedagogical in nature:

- Does the composition teach?
- What does it teach?
- What do your students need?
- Will the knowledge they gain from the composition be transferable?
- Does the composition challenge your students technically?
- Does the piece have aesthetic value?

As we consider "The Stars and Stripes Forever," we can create a list of several aspects of the work that demonstrate its quality as a composition—including its place in American music history, technical challenges for all sections of the ensemble, a prime example of American march form, and exploring notions of patriotism. This forms a foundation from which we can then further analyze the work pedagogically and begin to construct outcomes and strategies, using the CMP framework.

ANALYSIS

This analysis consists of an examination of the selected composition and the way in which it is organized. Musical analysis is a focus in undergraduate coursework and forms the foundation for careful score study, a necessary part of the rehearsal process. However, the process of analysis within the CMP model looks at the selected composition through a wide-angle lens, in that the analysis serves to identify major structural elements, harmonic organization, and key center, as opposed to a chord-by-chord harmonic analysis. Key questions include identifying tonality, motivic material, and compositional devices. The purpose of the analysis is to identify distinctive aspects that can be taught through the selected piece.

This analysis often leads to the development of learning goals or outcomes. This approach to analysis is unique in that the analysis informs the teaching of the work (the music); for this reason, we shall refer to the process as a pedagogical analysis. We begin by asking, "What kind of piece is this?" Let's look at "Arirang," a folk song from Korea, as an example.

As we examine the melody, we notice that it is a folk song that uses the pentatonic scale. We also discover the phrase structure as A A B A, the melodic contour, and the use of dotted-quarter-eighth note rhythmic motive. These details begin to reveal aspects of the piece, in this case a simple folk song, that can inform our teaching. For example, the use of the pentatonic scale carries many possibilities, from studying other works that use that particular scale to aspects of non-Western music to opportunities for composition using a pentatonic scale.

The question "what kind of piece is this?" provides a doorway into the process of analysis. As we dig deeper, we take note of other features of the work, using a series of guided questions. To make the process a bit more rigorous, we will refer to "The Stars and Stripes Forever." The questions are selected from the CMP workshop planning documents mentioned earlier (see appendix B).

- How are the musical elements utilized? Consider melody, form, harmony, timbre, rhythm, texture, expression.
- What compositional devices are used?
- What combination of musical ideas leads to this being a quality composition?
- What makes it worth rehearsing and performing?
- What historical connections or learnings can you draw from the composition?

Arirang

folk song from Korea

10

Figure 2.2. "Arirang"

Our exemplar piece, "The Stars and Stripes Forever," is constructed in American march form: First strain (A), second strain (B), trio (C), break strain (D and C1). The key is E-flat major until the trio, where one flat is added (in keeping with this distinct form). The first and second strains are peppered with accents, the trio is legato, and the break strain combines both styles. Use of timbre and texture varies in each strain. The compositional devices used are not especially sophisticated; rather, the work is a model of balance in unity and variety (use of diatonic passages alternated with chromaticism, for example) in a pristine construction. The question of historical connections has been addressed earlier. Within the realm of American music, "The Stars and Stripes Forever" is a classic work.

One of the key components in the analysis process using the CMP model is to identify the *heart* of the selected composition. Discovering the heart of the selected piece provides an opportunity to analyze the affective rather than merely technical aspects of the music. O'Toole (2003, p. 18) presents several questions that can lead to the identification of the heart of a selected composition, including:

- What attracted you to this piece of music?
- What maintains your interest in it?
- What gives this piece its distinctive qualities?

In the CMP model, the heart of the piece is a distinctive way of thinking about analysis as we determine that aspect of the work that draws us in, brings us back, holds our interest. What is a quality of a particular piece that serves as a center? Its driving force? This is often derived from the musical elements and is personally constructed by the teacher. According to O'Toole, "there can be a number of reasons that attract you to a piece of music, so the heart is not only the sustaining attractive elements, but also that quality that makes a piece of music distinct" (2003, p. 18). For example, the heart of the first movement, "Chaconne," in Holst's *First Suite in E-flat for Military Band*, could be "the unity created by repetition of a simple melody contrasted with imaginative variations" (p. 20). In "The Stars and Stripes Forever," for example, one might consider the feelings of patriotism that the work evokes as the heart of the piece. The heart of a composition is distinctly individual and often varies from one person to another. It can be a challenging way to consider a composition; at the same time, it opens up an affective dimension, expanding our view of the piece.

As we work through our analysis of the Sousa, we take note of key matters such as its classic march form, historical importance (of the work and of this composer), precise articulations, and chromatic passages. This information, then, will be quite useful as we move through the process to outcomes.

Additional support for the importance of using analysis to inform the planning of comprehensive music teaching is encouraged by Demorest (1996), and he describes this as the first step in planning a rehearsal. In addition to addressing the questions listed above, he encourages the teacher-conductor to locate the "natural breaks" in a piece as an aid to organize the rehearsal. This approach may also help with balancing this kind of detailed study within the daily rehearsal and its myriad tasks.

OUTCOMES

Outcomes are learning goals; those things that the teacher wants students to know or be able to do. The primary question when determining specific learning goals remains the same: *What do you want students to learn?* Leonhard and House (1972) provide a detailed description of learning goals informed by Bloom's Taxonomy. Among their classification of outcomes are knowledge, skill, understanding, attitudes, and appreciations. The intentional curriculum is informed by outcomes or learning goals that identify specific knowledge and behaviors that students are to attain. Among those outcomes identified by Labuta (1997) are general styles of music, musical phrasing, historical styles, and musical affect.

Within the CMP model, there are three types of outcomes. Skill outcomes address matters of technical proficiency. An example of a skill outcome related to "The Stars and Stripes Forever" might be: The students will perform written articulations with accuracy. A second type of outcome is cognitive, which is designed to help students gain musical knowledge. For example: The students will identify and name facts about John Philip Sousa and his work. This outcome is an example of one that helps broaden the understanding of the work beyond technicalities of notes and rhythms. The use of knowledge outcomes has been emphasized by Garofalo (1983) and Labuta (1997) as an essential component of a comprehensive musical experience in band. A third type of outcome within the CMP model is affective outcomes. Affective outcomes are a distinct component of CMP and seek to address the subjective dimension of the musical experience. Abeles, Hoffer, and Klotman (1995) provide several useful guidelines for teaching sensitivity to and awareness of aesthetic qualities of music. They use the "Air" from Bach's Suite No. 3 for Orchestra (often referred to as "Air on the G String"). An example in pursuit of the affective could include a consideration of the ways the piece arouses the senses—such as the opening whole note, often played with a crescendo. The authors pose a question designed to discover the aesthetic features of a composition: "What about the piece makes it interesting and attractive to listen to?" (1995, p. 84). This seemingly simple question could be asked of every piece in the ensemble folder.

Affective outcomes are often located in the personal knowledge of the individual student. They may be less tangible and measurable than the other types of outcomes, but they are equally important (O'Toole, 2003). An example of an affective/personal knowledge outcome might be: "The students will explore themes of consonance and dissonance, both in music and in their personal relationships" (p. 39). Among the categories of affective outcomes are student relationships (to the music, to each other or the world, to himself or herself) which build community and the composer's craft. For example, consider "The Stars and Stripes Forever." This work often evokes feelings of patriotism. We could construct an affective outcome by asking students to describe the ways Sousa uses music to evoke patriotism and follow up with a discussion of what patriotism means. This kind of affective outcome speaks to both the composer's craft and the student's relationship to the world. *Shaping Sound Musicians* includes several useful examples of affective outcomes.

In the CMP model, the heart statement often leads to affective outcomes, as illustrated in the previous example. Among the many examples of comprehensive musicianship, knowledge and skill development are universal—however, the affective dimension is often missing from the music curricula in general. For many teachers, constructing the affective outcome presents the greatest challenge; yet this often yields most satisfying results, as illustrated in the vignettes from Mr. Gabriel's classroom. The CMP planning process elevates affective outcomes by including them in the teaching plan.

Long-Term Outcomes

An additional consideration in relation to outcomes is the long view. We have discussed in detail outcomes designed for teaching a particular piece—a course of study that would typically fill several weeks. In a longer view, teachers need to be mindful of long-term outcomes and goals of their program. That is to say, beyond the scope of a single concert, what are the goals of the music program over the course of a school year? Over multiple years? Perhaps more weighty, long-term goals that forward a lifelong involvement in music as a performer, listener, and creator. One example of a longer-reaching outcome comes from the classroom of a middle school band room: "Students will explore, define, and personalize a concept of excellence to use in their study of music during the first quarter of the band curriculum" (Sindberg, 2006, p. 186). This example is discussed in detail in chapter 6.

Clandinin and Connelly also talk about outcomes, in relation to a project they did bringing narrative inquiry and Bloom's Taxonomy together. "Let us take an example of a common woodworking tool, a lathe. A lathe is a tool useful to different people, at different times, in different contexts. It is useful to commercial woodworkers, to hobbyists, to woodworking tool manufacturers, to students and so on; in factories, in small home hobby shops, in schools, and so on" (2000, p. 26). Clandinin and Connelly's characterization reinforces the pairing of distinct uses or tools with shared intentions. A similar example from a music classroom or ensemble could be performing with expression.

Transfer

Transfer of learning includes the effect of learned skills, knowledge, or understanding on later learning of other skills, knowledge, or understanding, and is an important part of the teaching and learning process because it helps students apply knowledge across musical contexts. When students make associations between a focus of study and something else and transfer their knowledge from one piece to another, this is particularly valuable evidence of learning (Sindberg, 2006).

How can we give conscious consideration to transfer as we plan instruction? In the CMP model, we ask if a particular outcome will transfer from one piece to another: *Is this outcome transferable?* A simple yes or no is not enough if we want to ensure transfer of knowledge from one piece or context to another. What is needed is a mechanism or strategy to help students transfer learnings. Outcomes designed with transfer in mind help lead students toward musical understanding, described by Leonhard and House (1972) as an application of knowledge by a learner toward new experiences and learning. Various definitions of musical understanding show a dynamic quality and an interdependence—evolving and changing as students engage in various learning activities and experiences, dependent upon what is already known by the individual learner. Transfer of outcomes is a link that facilitates understanding, and a necessary component of the planning process. A description of how we will assist students with the transfer of learning from one work to another is a necessary component in this planning process.

STRATEGIES

Good teachers develop a repertoire of strategies for helping their students, which is informed by their personal practical knowledge—that knowing of a classroom that is particular to each individual. Introduced by Connelly and

Clandinin, this form of knowledge is manifested in the way the teacher approaches the many facets of teaching and planning instruction (1988). This comes to life during the teaching process, as the teacher balances his or her use of planned strategies with the spontaneity that is a part of the life of the dynamic classroom.

Strategies are the series of steps or activities that will lead to the achievement of the selected outcome. Strategies involve different types of student engagement. Strategies involve a range of activities, including some traditionally found in performing ensembles and others less typical in those settings, such as composition, journal writing, and listening activities. To illustrate, I restate an outcome from an earlier paragraph: *The students will identify the compositional devices used in this composition.* Sample strategies might include (1) students identify different sections by raising their hand when something changes in the piece; (2) students describe the way the composer creates change in the composition; (3) students draw a picture of the form of the composition; (4) students listen to a piece composed in similar form and describe what is the same and what is different. The strategies, then, are the various activities or steps that lead to the student being able to ultimately describe what the composer has done.

Often referred to as the playground of the CMP model, strategies are those steps that lead students to achievement of our outcomes. It is in this area, strategies, where the creativity of the teacher is engaged. Strategies are an outgrowth of outcomes and address the "how" of music teaching. They articulate a sequence of instruction.

One way to begin the process of writing strategies is to have an outcome in mind, and from that outcome simply brainstorm several ideas for strategies. For example, students could look at the piano reduction of "The Stars and Stripes Forever" and identify various sections of the work. They could listen to recordings of the work with the same intention—to identify the form of the piece. Students could also listen to various recordings (wind band, orchestra, chamber ensemble) and compare each. All of these strategies engage students as musicians and provide opportunities toward student ownership as responses are shared among the ensemble. Another strategy related to understanding form could be for students to compose a work that either replicates march form or is in a contrasting form. If students have limited experience with composition, they can work in groups and create a rhythmic work. The development of strategies is really limited only by the teacher's imagination. In this way, strategies help to free the creativity of the teacher, breathing vitality into the rehearsal. Generally, it's advisable to have three to five strategies for each outcome.

The importance of using strategies that are varied and address different learning styles has been a tenet in music classrooms for many years. Teachers need to reflect on the ways in which they learn as well as how others learn. Teachers tend to teach how they learn best; this is not always in line with the way students learn. For example, a teacher who feels he is primarily a visual learner may need to make a greater effort to devise effective strategies for students who learn aurally. If an ensemble is rehearsing a folk song, effective strategies could include both reading songs and performing them by ear. In another example, the use of Curwen[1] hand signs not only helps students who may have an affinity to kinesthetic learning, but can also assist in understanding placement of scale degrees. A conscious approach to planning varied strategies will help all students.

Strategies provide opportunities for students to participate as musicians—one of the central tenets of the original comprehensive musicianship initiatives: to develop an understanding and competency of all areas of music through the integration of performing, creating/composing, conducting, listening to, and discussing music. Comprehensive musicianship involves students in a variety of roles including performing, improvising, composing, transcribing, arranging, conducting, rehearsing, and visually and aurally analyzing music (Wisconsin Music Educators Association, 1977).

Perhaps most importantly, strategies are an effective vehicle toward establishing a student-centered classroom and a way to move away from a teacher-centric classroom; it also echoes Wersen's long-ago call for students to take ownership of their own musical growth (1968). Such a shift has been supported by many authors but has not consistently come to life in the band, choir, and orchestra rehearsal. Strategies that foster more student engagement can be a stepping-stone toward reforming the ensemble setting into a more collaborative and dynamic learning environment that will not compromise musical performance. Student-led warm-ups, chamber groups, and goal setting are three examples of student-centered strategies. Varied, engaging, and meaningful strategies can forward a comprehensive, deeper musical experience that combines musical performance with broader learning with students at the center.

ASSESSMENT

Analyzing music, organizing outcomes, and devising strategies are important steps in the planning process. Having a plan is one thing; finding out to what extent that plan is working is another. Taking steps to discover to what extent students have (or have not) learned what we have been teaching is essential and has been addressed in many educational publications. In this section we consider assessment of teaching and learning.

Arts PROPEL was one initiative that shed new light on assessment in the arts, through a reexamination of instruction and evaluation of student learning. This created a shift from testing to a broader view as the project sought to "make students' learning more visible to the students themselves and to others and, in turn, to make the assessment process itself foster further learning" (ed. Winner, 1995, p. 5).

In recent years, *assessment* has become a significant issue in education, particularly in matters of accountability and resulting in creating varied interpretations of what is meant by it. Because of the many interpretations of assessment and related terms, it is helpful to clarify working definitions of those terms, as used in this text.

Assessment—gathering information about student learning

Evaluation—making a judgment about the information gathered

Measurement—quantifying information gathered and judgments into a grade

Authentic assessment—tasks that are part of the real-world experience (ex. composing a melody or performing a solo)

Formative assessment—tasks that are intertwined with the educational process (ex. rehearsal or individual practice)

Summative assessment—includes tasks designed to evaluate student progress (ex. solo performance)

Assessment needs to take place before, during, and after teaching—assessment and evaluation of learning and teaching is an ongoing process. It represents how the teacher discovers to what extent students have achieved a selected outcome. For example, we may consider selecting a particular composition based on certain things our students need to learn. If we refer to "The Stars and Stripes Forever," we recognize that this composition can provide technical challenges for students as well as an opportunity to learn about John Philip Sousa. During the rehearsal, the teacher-conductor embeds assessment tasks to evaluate student learning and performance over several weeks. Assessment is tailored to various outcomes and related specifically to the strategies planned by the teacher, and is most useful when both teacher and student participate in the evaluative measures. For example, if the ensemble is working to clarify articulation, invite students to participate by evaluating their performance, either individually or as an ensemble. Both are important in mastering articulation skills; they also are a function of assessment.

Our goal is to embed assessment into the rehearsal so that it becomes a part of the routine as an integral and dynamic part of the teaching and learning process. The challenge in the music ensemble is to gather information about student learning effectively. Traditionally, teacher-conductors observe student performances within the large group. We make assumptions based on these large-scale observations, and those assumptions are risky. Just because a student looks like he or she is playing his or her part does not tell the full story; we need to pursue the accuracy with which that individual is performing.

There are many, many ways to assess teaching and learning—examples that have been shared by several authors, including Farrell (2000) and Music Educators National Conference (1996). Just as we seek to provide a variety of teaching strategies, we need to include a variety of assessment tasks. These tasks can be completed relatively quickly, as in the case of a three-by-five card on which students describe what they learned from "The Stars and Stripes Forever"; over a period of several days in which students complete a study sheet with several questions related to a particular composition; or through a more detailed essay-writing assignment in which students describe their perceptions or beliefs about patriotism.

A discussion of assessment naturally has implications for grading. More thorough assessments can lead to informed grading, which in the music classroom can be particularly challenging. If our grades can be informed by comprehensive, relevant assessment tasks that engage students, they will be more meaningful for students. Students can be invited into the process through something as simple as a narrative describing their growth and accomplishments over the past several weeks, or they can complete a prepared self-evaluation sheet that asks specific questions, such as the example below, completed by a grade 8 band student (figure 2.3).

Viewed within the context of the CMP model, assessment represents how the teacher discovers to what extent students have achieved the selected outcome. Teachers can collect evidence of musical growth and teaching effectiveness in varied ways as described earlier. From the standpoint of assessment, the assessment pieces I have used in my CMP practice have enabled me to locate evidence of student growth and understanding. I believe this is true because the assessment activities invite every single student to respond, to contribute, often in written form—this is far more revealing than the more typical raising of hands.

Thoughtful attention will lead to assessment becoming a routine part of the rehearsal and part of the learning process on a regular basis. In addition to determining competency with regard to basic skills, assessments should help students develop critical thinking and communication of ideas in relation to musical experiences. Rather than considering assessment a final product, think of it more as an episode of learning as suggested by Wolf (1991). Categories such as authentic, performance, summative and formative can help organize tasks and communicate with others—the key is to be purposeful about assessment.

In evaluating your work in Band over the past nine weeks, consider the following:

APPROACH TO WORK:
Did you work consistently each day? Why or why not? What was your level of effort outside of class (i.e. home practice)? How did you contribute to our group?

I think that I worked consistently each day and tried to do my best. I practiced around 120 min. each week at home. I tried to contribute a good sound and attitude to our group.

QUALITY OF WORK—IMPROVEMENT AND GROWTH
In what ways did you grow musically this quarter? What improvements did you make? Did you work on your ensemble and perform it at a high musical level, or did you just learn the notes? Did you do any extra work?

I grew musically this quarter by learning how all elements of music need to be there for a good piece. I did very well at solo/ensemble and performed my ensemble to my best ability w/ correct dynamics,

MUSICAL UNDERSTANDING *rhythms etc. I did very well on my solo + worked*
Hopefully, as the year progresses, you learn more about the elements of music and you increase *hard f*
your musical understanding. What did you learn about the elements of music? *it.*

Again, I learned that all of the elements have to be there for a piece to sound good. Also, I learned that dynamics are imp.

CODA *to give a piece a certain mood/feeling.*

Please include here anything else that will help Ms. Sindberg to know and understand you and your accomplishments.

I enjoy band and try to perform to my best ability. I worked hard here & at home!

GRADES *(I ♡ the French Horn ♡)*
In consideration of your responses to these questions, what grade did you earn this quarter? Include a separate grade for your work in your ensemble project.

A
QUARTER GRADE   ENSEMBLE GRADE *A*   *continued*

Figure 2.3. Student Self-Assessment

MUSIC SELECTION, REVISITED

Having examined the discrete components of the CMP model, we return to the music selection with "new" eyes. Among the questions posed from the standpoint of the teacher-conductor are, "Will I have enough time to prepare the music for performance? Is it too easy? Too hard? What do my students need? Do I have the instruments or voices to perform this piece? Will the students like the music? Will I like the music?" And in a broader context, "How does this piece fit within other pieces selected? Does it complement or lend variety in terms of a balanced blend of styles or technical challenges? How does it fit within a larger, more far-reaching outcome?"

The selection of repertoire represents philosophical decisions on the part of the teacher-conductor as well as significant personal investment. We look closely at a score and work to assess its pedagogical merits, value, craft, beauty, design, and appeal. We often then become attached to this work and excited to share it with students. From their point of view, the appeal of this work may not be immediately apparent, and this is often where the process can sink or swim. Knowing a piece and all it has to offer students is our responsibility, as is keeping our eye on the long view as the students struggle with what may seem tedious and impossible. Not all students will love "Ave Verum Corpus"[2] at first; but over time, as students gain an understanding of the work, it becomes something meaningful and memorable. Since the CMP model bases the ensemble curriculum in repertoire, standards for choosing high-quality works are paramount.

Another critical component of this process is to pursue the selection of quality repertoire and to strike a balance between the many variables that inform repertoire selection. Students in the ensembles are often eager to perform the recent popular tunes, in whatever simplified version they are published. Teachers need to weigh those wishes in light of the broader lens of the curriculum. This is not to say the use of popular music is inconsistent with principles and practices of Comprehensive Musicianship through Performance; rather, each teacher is responsible for making choices that best suit the particular teaching situation. The questions pose in the first paragraph of this section will aid in the process.

THE CMP TEACHING PLAN

The CMP teaching plan is a document that encapsulates the planning process, including all points of the model. The teaching plan template has been modified over the years by members of the CMP Committee as well as by individual teachers who adapt the template to fit their situations. Depending on the individual teacher, this teaching plan can range in length from a few to several pages. What remains consistent is the inclusion of material related to each point of the model.

From that teaching plan, the teacher selects strategies to employ during a single rehearsal, which typically includes several pieces—the CMP teaching plan work and other compositions. This addresses matters of enactment, which is discussed in chapter 5. An abbreviated form of the teaching plan template is provided below, in table 2.1. Additional

Table 2.1. CMP Teaching Plan (Abbreviated)

Title:
Composer:
Arranger or Editor:
Music selection—describe what makes this piece a valuable teaching piece and musical work.
Analysis
Broad description, type/genre
Background information
Additional information (choral/instrumental)
Elements of music
    Form
    Rhythm
    Melody
    Harmony
    Timbre
    Texture
    Expression

What is the heart of this piece?
List one strategy for introducing the work
Outcomes, followed by Strategies
Skill outcome:
1.
2.
3.
Knowledge outcome:
1.
2.
3.
Affective outcome:
1.
2.
3.

Assessment—list one assessment task for each outcome
Skill
Knowledge
Affective

musical examples are included in the appendix and serve to demonstrate how different teacher-conductors construct a teaching plan.

CONCLUSION

Writing a CMP teaching plan is an exercise in planning during which we delineate each point of the model; we separate the points so that we can organize and plot our intentions. Although fairly detailed, the process also invites the creativity of the teacher in the development of strategies; it also is grounded in the repertoire selected by the teacher as a foundation for development musical understanding through performance in the ensemble. Additional examples of CMP teaching plans are included in the appendix as a way of displaying varied methods for constructing the plan. Each plan includes the discrete points of the CMP model; what varies is the level of detail and organizational layout.

GOING FURTHER—QUESTIONS FOR DISCUSSION

1. In what ways is the CMP model different from or similar to ways music teachers have planned and taught music in the past?
2. Labuta said, "The music presents the problems, the solutions develop musicianship." What does this really say? How do music teachers develop musicianship for themselves and for their students?
3. In what ways does a CMP analysis differ from a traditional approach to score analysis?
4. What are the differences between larger outcomes in a CMP teaching plan and smaller outcomes that occur more frequently? Give examples.
5. Select a score and apply it to the abbreviated version of the CMP teaching plan template. What do you notice about the study and planning process at this level?

NOTES

1. Often used in the Kodály method, Curwen hand signs are visual cues used to represent different scale degrees.
2. This hymn has been set by several composers, perhaps the most well known of whom is Mozart. It has been arranged for band, orchestra, and of course, choral settings. This context refers to an arrangement of Mozart's work used in a school setting.

3

"Shenandoah" Viewed from a Choral and Instrumental Perspective

The history of this well-known and widely sung song, like that of so many others, is an illusive and tantalizing will-o'-the-wisp. One follows a promising clue only to find that the end of one trail is but the beginning of another . . . (Lomax, 1994, p. 543).

WHY "SHENANDOAH"? ONE PIECE, TWO CLASSROOMS, AND THREE OUTCOMES

"Shenandoah" has been a much-loved song for generations. Although like many folk songs its origins are un-known, the lilting melody, message of longing, and general nostalgia combine to inspire a transcendent musical experience. Known and treasured by many, "Shenandoah" has often been included in school music programs: a recent search of publications listed arrangements for chorus, solo voice, concert band, beginning band, orchestra, marching band, and a host of chamber configurations as well as piano and guitar. Another anecdotal measure of a musical work's popularity can be the number of versions available on iTunes. For "Shenandoah," that numbers nearly 200!

As with many folk songs, "Shenandoah" is not comprised of a single, definitive text or origin. It has been assigned to the Shenandoah River; others suggest Native American origins in the telling of a daughter of the Indian chief Shenandoah, who is courted by a white Missouri river trader over a period of seven years (Library of Congress, Song of America Project, downloaded from http://www.loc.gov/creativity/hampson/about_shenandoah.html). In *The Folk Songs of North America*, Lomax speculates that "Shenandoah" began as a voyageur song on the rivers west of the Mississippi, "taking its title from the Indians for whom the great valley of Virginia was named" (1975, p. 37). According to Lomax, the song later became popular with the cavalry who often fought the Indians out west but who also fell in love with and married Indian women. Lomax calls "Shenandoah" the most beautiful of all the sea songs in English. The song first appeared in print in *Harper's New Monthly* magazine in 1882, in an article by William L. Alden (also available through the Song of America Project). This background information provides rich material as we examine "Shenandoah" with an eye toward comprehensiveness.

In this chapter we will use "Shenandoah" as the point from which to explore the Comprehensive Musicianship through Performance (CMP) model and create a teaching plan. Whether approaching this work from a choral or instrumental perspective, using the melody and text as starting points we can construct outcomes that will transfer between the two types of ensembles. Some of the strategies and assessments will also be transferable; others will be specific to the choral or instrumental setting. The idea of looking at a single work that speaks to multiple applications helps demonstrate two important aspects of the CMP model: as a framework that speaks multiple dialects (band, choir, orchestra) and as a tool that gives voice to the creativity of the individual teacher. This CMP teaching plan includes each of the five points of the model, described in chapter 2.

Shenandoah

Figure 3.1. "Shenandoah"

"SHENANDOAH" TEACHING PLAN

Background

Few sea chanteys originated in this country since we were a brand new nation in the days of sailing vessels, but "Shenandoah" is genuinely American, according to Lomax (1975). The song seems to have originated in the early nineteenth century as a land ballad in the areas of the Mississippi and Missouri Rivers, with a story of a trader who fell in love with the daughter of the Indian Chief Shenandoah. This enchanting song was taken up by sailors plying these rivers in keel and Mackinaw boats, and thus made its way down the Mississippi to the open ocean. The song had great appeal for American deep-sea sailors, and its rolling melody made it ideal as a capstan chantey, where a group of sailors push the massive capstan bars around and around in order to lift the heavy anchor.

The song reached its first height of popularity perhaps a little before the 1840s, the beginning of the fast clipper ship era that added so much to American growth. The song was traditional with the U.S. Army cavalry who called it "The Wild Mizzourye."

When steamboats replaced the sailing vessels, sailors and landlubbers alike were reluctant to give up this best-of-all-chanteys, and so it has remained to this day one of our most beautiful and popular folk songs (Raph, 1964, p. 81).

These CMP teaching plans are based on arrangements by James Erb (SSAATTBB, a cappella), published by Alfred (1975) and Frank Ticheli (concert band), published by Manhattan Beach Music (1999). While one arrangement is for voices and one for instruments, the teaching plans are conceptualized in a way that illustrates the fluidity of the CMP model. The analysis of this piece is unified in the original melody; however, each composer incorporates the other musical elements in a distinct way. The three outcomes can be used in a choral or instrumental setting, as can many of the strategies. In this example, then, we see how a song that is as inherently beautiful, rich, and expressive as "Shenandoah" can form the basis of a CMP teaching plan with universal application. The points of the CMP model appear in the following order: analysis, outcomes, strategies, assessment, and music selection. In the analysis section, distinctions are made between Erb and Ticheli's works. Score excerpts are included to illustrate aspects of the analysis. Full scores are available from the publishers.

Analysis

Melody

The melody of "Shenandoah" is diatonic, moving equally in steps and skips. The melodic structure is two four-bar phrases and a two-bar coda, organized in two-bar "chunks"—a-b-a-c. The "a" phrases are less active, in contrast to the "b" phrase, which begins a 6th higher than the "a" phrase ends. The "c" phrase is the most reflective and restful of the four. The melodic shape contributes to the sense of longing: longing is inherent in the rise of the opening phrase and the subsequent fall at the end of the phrase. Also, the second phrase begins on a higher pitch and descends on the word "away," which suggests longing as is expressed in the human language through a cry or a sigh. The rhythm of the four-measure phrases is very similar but not identical. While the text of each verse changes, the words to the coda remain the same: "across the wide Missouri." Whether singing or playing an arrangement of "Shenandoah," the text plays a central role in the sense of longing and understanding of the meaning and expression. The range of the melody is an octave + perfect 4th. Ticheli's work also includes an original melody introduced in measure 23.

Harmony

- Erb—Erb's arrangement is in E major throughout. It is diatonic, and understated—again, in keeping with the style of folk music in general and this folk tune in particular. Rather than a complex harmonic structure, Erb uses fragments of the melody and text to create harmony, causing harmony and rhythm to be closely tied. Harmonic development occurs through repeated eighth notes, often moving stepwise. Erb repeats selected portions of the melody, which creates an echo, reinforcing a notion of longing. Erb makes frequent use of the perfect fourth as a harmonic device. Erb's use of suspension is subtle and sparse. A close canon in m. 32–41 (figure 3.2) echoes the ebb and flow of a river, through the layering of the women's entrances, an effect that Erb maintains until the end of the work. It is the echo of the melody in this canon, in combination with the text, that reinforces the notion of longing.

- Ticheli—Ticheli's composition begins in E-flat and uses G-flat as a transition to B-flat in the development section before returning to E-flat at the recapitulation (again via G-flat). Ticheli's use of harmonic devices is relatively uncomplicated in that it is largely diatonic (perhaps because it is based on a folk song). Rather than relying on simple block chords, however, Ticheli employs a more linear approach to harmony; rhythmic activity of the accompanying figures as the piece progresses. For example, in m. 23 (figure 3.3) Ticheli introduces a second theme, loosely based on the folk song. The accompaniment is comprised of slurred quarter notes, grouped in fours and in a sequence that gradually moves up and then down over several measures. Harmonic devices include not only chords, but frequent use of rhythmic motives, including stepwise slurred quarter notes grouped in twos and fours—as if to represent the movement of a river, as in the text, "rolling river" and "wide Missouri." One can imagine, while hearing this harmonic device, the word rolling, rolling, over and over. These insistent quarter notes may suggest breath. In m. 56 drama builds with Ticheli's use of layers: melody, pulsating quarter notes, "glory, glory, hallelujah" countermelody, and eighth notes cascading downward. Ticheli's infrequent use of harmonic suspensions makes them particularly potent, like a taste of wasabi before it dissipates on the tongue.

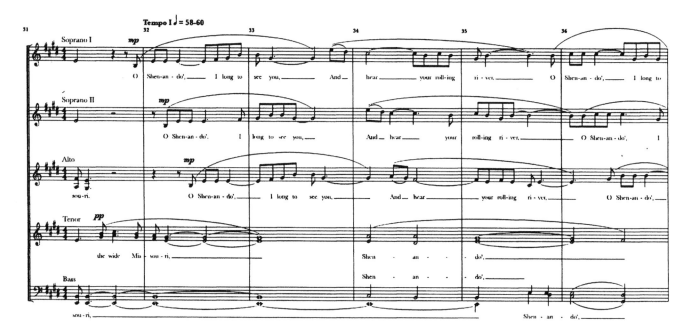

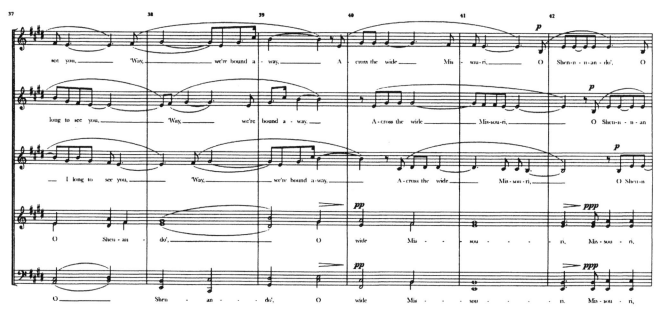

Figure 3.2. Erb, m. 32–41

Figure 3.3.   Ticheli, m. 23–31

Form

- Erb—This arrangement of "Shenandoah" includes three verses and a transition to a brief development followed by a coda. This is an uncomplicated arrangement that reflects the simplicity of the folk song. Each verse is eight bars long with a two-bar coda.

m. 1–10   Verse one—soprano and alto in unison

m. 11–20   Verse two—tenor and bass in unison

m. 21–32   Verse three—soprano melody, alto, tenor, bass accompaniment in block chords. Verse three is extended with an echo of "the wide Missouri."

m. 32–41   Development—repetition of the first verse in close canon in women's voices. Block chords support the canon, combining movement and stability.

m. 42–47   Coda—repetition of "Shenandoah," both in canon in women's voices and in block chords in men's voices. Piece ends with a repetition of the opening motive sung in male falsetto.

- Ticheli—"Shenandoah" is constructed in sonata form: exposition, development, recapitulation. Transitions accompany each shift to a new section. A description of the organizational framework follows:

m. 1–11   First statement of the melody (verse one), presented in the horns and euphonium. Accompaniment is in clarinets.

m. 12–22   Second statement of the melody (verse two). Trumpets—melody, accompaniment in upper woodwinds, echoing fragments of the melody. Low brass and low woodwinds provide harmony through sustained notes with slight movement.

m. 23–30   Introduction of second B theme, an original theme based on the melody of "Shenandoah," presented in flute and alto sax—response part in muted trumpet.

m. 31–55   Transition to the development. Pulsating quarter-note ostiano implies rolling river or heartbeat. Key changes to G-flat. Portions of the B theme are presented in the horns and are followed by a three-part close canon in the flutes beginning in m. 41–50. In m. 51, Ticheli begins a transition from B-flat to E-flat via G-flat, a somewhat unusual harmonic path. As the development progresses, fragments of the original melody and B theme are included.

m. 56–68   Recapitulation (verse three), return to original key of E-flat. Melody is now in several voices; pulsating quarter notes continue as if to evoke ebb and flow of a river; expression also becomes more active with use of dynamics and accents as the climax of the piece approaches. Ticheli also inserts a quote of the refrain of the "Battle Hymn of the Republic" ("glory, glory hallelujah") in the horns and alto sax, perhaps as a tribute to the person to whom this piece is dedicated. The climax of the work occurs in m. 60: fortissimo, accents, tutti, last statement of "She-nan-do . . . "

m. 69–78   Coda—Brass chorale creates a feeling of reverence. In measure 73 the horn issues a final call, perhaps another prompt inspired by the young man for whom this piece was created. Ticheli characterizes this section as a "kind of prayer—a moment of deep reflection (Ticheli, 1999)." The closing expression marking in low brass and clarinets is *niente*.

Rhythm

- Erb—This is not a highly rhythmic piece; however, the rhythm of the piece tries to capture the idea of a flowing river. One repeated rhythmic motive is the eighth note as anacrusis. Each phrase of the melody has an anacrusis. When the melody has long notes, Erb provides rhythmic motion with moving notes in other parts, often stepwise alternating notes; this creates a wavelike feeling. Rhythm in the canonic section overlaps by a quarter note each instance—a very close canon. The tempo of "Shenandoah" is slow: quarter note equals 58–60, and is slightly slower in verse three. The original tempo returns at m. 32.

- Ticheli—The melody of "Shenandoah" is rhythmically simple: quarter notes, eighth notes, and half notes. Each phrase of the melody begins with a pickup, either a quarter note or half note; several notes are tied. While this piece is not rhythmically challenging, Ticheli creates interest by using rhythms derived from the melody to provide and sustain motion. The most common device he employs is the addition of layers and melodic fragments as countermelody figures when the melody is sustained. Rhythm is used for pulse in the way a river ebbs and flows—for example, in m. 35–40 (figure 3.4). In the development section (beginning in m. 35) the use of rhythm is more static; motion is provided through pulsating quarter notes slurred in twos. Rhythmic figures are not individually complex; complexity results from Ticheli's layering of simple rhythms throughout the piece.

Figure 3.4.   Ticheli, m. 35–40

Timbre

- Erb—This arrangement is a cappella, for eight-part chorus: SSAATTBB. The overall effect of the timbre is subtle and pure, and the result of the masterful use of the arranger's manipulation of voicing. Erb groups women's voices, then men's voices, and then combines both in verse three. Because the melody is the same, Erb creates variety by altering the voicings—having women present verse one in unison and men present verse two in unison. At the coda, m. 42–47 (figure 3.5), a pedal tone is sustained in the male voices; an interesting static contrast. At the end of the piece Erb returns to the simple beginnings of his piece; however, here those opening notes are sung falsetto in the male voices—the result is a familiar yet striking difference in color. "Shenandoah" begins in unison and ends in unison.

- Ticheli—Ticheli does not shy away from tonal variety; there is lots of contrast in tone color throughout "Shenandoah." Each presentation of the theme is distinct in timbre. For example, the dark, rich sounds of the horn and euphonium in the opening verse are contrasted with moments of light of the flute canon that begins in m. 41 ("ethereal, floating"). The horns are a prominent voice in this work, perhaps because the young man to whom it is dedicated was a horn player. The use of solo alto saxophone, flute, and muted trumpet are among the devices Ticheli employs to provide timbral contrast. As with many works by Ticheli, the colors of the wind band are exploited in imaginative ways while also incorporating standard scoring practices (e.g., woodwind and brass groupings), in keeping with the level of this particular piece (grade 3 on a scale of 1 to 6). Percussion provides color and accentuates new sections—for example, the use of the triangle to highlight the new melody at m. 23; the use of chimes in m. 35 (see figure 3.4) punctuates the beginning of the development section just before the horns present their portion of the B theme ("stately, exalted"), adding dimension to this section.

Figure 3.5. Erb, m. 42–47

Texture

- Erb—Grows in complexity, moving from unison (verses one and two) to a use of layers. Erb creates contrast as he increases the number of layers beginning with the third verse in m. 21 (figure 3.6). Here, he presents the melody in the soprano part and accompaniment in block chords in the alto, tenor, and bass parts. In this verse he also varies the texture by repeating fragments of the text, particularly "rolling river" and "Shenando'." The result is increased activity. The canon that begins in m. 32 balances the unity of the melody with variety in the treatment of that melody, in this case a close canon in three parts. Block chords provide stability in contrast to the canon in the soprano and alto voices.

- Ticheli—Ticheli begins the piece simply, with melody and accompaniment—an accompaniment that includes two layers—a slow countermelody in the low woodwinds and sustained chord tones in the low voices. With each repetition of the melody, Ticheli adds layers, many of which are fragments of the original melody. At m. 69 (figure 3.7) Ticheli includes a brief chorale, and "Shenandoah" concludes as it began—simply—with echoes of the perfect 4th that begins the original melody and its inversion, the perfect 5th. Instrumentation is greatly varied, with balance of tutti and combinations of soloistic passages.

Figure 3.6.   Erb, m. 21–30

Ticheli, m. 69–78

Expression

- Erb—The expressive character of this work is gentle, understated, caressing. Erb uses a range of dynamics from *ppp* to *f*; however, forte is used only twice—in m. 5 and in m. 23, both as pickups to the second phrase of the melody. Dynamics in the canonic section are piano to pianissimo, evoking a feeling of distance, sentiment, and longing. A minimal use of dynamic markings allows the organic shape of the melody to be a primary expressive element of this piece. The harmony, whether in block chords or in a more active role, supports the melody throughout.

- Ticheli—"Shenandoah" is an inherently expressive tune. Ticheli enhances that with organic and subtle expressive devices. Dynamics are primarily on the soft end of the spectrum, making the climax at m. 60 particularly potent, through the use of ff, accents, and tutti instrumentation. Emphasis on softer dynamics will be a challenge for young players, both in execution and in terms of maintaining pitch. The bars just prior to and following the penultimate measure are very detailed and specific: accent, brief crescendo and decrescendo, tenuto, and sforzando. Very few accents are used, so when they are, it is quite effective. First accent occurs in m. 33; the next accent is in m. 48. Ticheli employs some perhaps unexpected adjectives as expressive devices: ethereal, floating, exalted, pulsating—these are intriguing terms that will engage the students' imaginations as they explore "Shenandoah." Ticheli's meticulous attention to expressive detail is among the most challenging aspects of this piece.

The Heart of "Shenandoah"

The heart of "Shenandoah" is the universal sense of longing, beautifully expressed in the melody and text, which evokes universal and enduring appeal.

As we work through our analysis of "Shenandoah," outcomes begin to emerge. Knowing that this piece is an American folk song, for example, immediately suggests an outcome that centers on that genre and its importance in music history. The next section of this chapter includes outcomes and strategies. The outcomes address skill development, knowledge, and affective domains.

Outcomes

Skill—Students will perform with smooth and expressive phrasing.

Cognitive—Students will identify and describe characteristics of folk music and explore its connections to other musical genres.

Affective—Students will explore the notion of nostalgia and how it is expressed in music and other art forms.

Strategies (Outcomes are restated and followed by related strategies.)

Skill—Students will perform with smooth and expressive phrasing.

1. In warm-ups, students will play or sing other folk song melodies with extended legato lines in unison (e.g., "Amazing Grace," "The Water Is Wide," "Wayfaring Stranger," "Streets of Laredo").
2. Have all students play or sing "Shenandoah" and invite selected students to conduct the piece in different ways to compare and contrast various ways for making something expressive. Discuss.
3. Hand out several written folk melodies to the ensemble. Students outline selected melodies and analyze the rise and fall of the phrase to demonstrate melodic contour.
4. Divide the ensemble into two groups. While playing or singing selected melodies, have students use large, arching arm motions to outline the melody.
5. Put a melody on the board and invite a student to add an expression marking. All play. Invite another student to add another expression marking and play the melody again. Repeat, adding expression markings as appropriate for the melody.
6. Play or sing "Shenandoah" with careful attention to phrasing. Have students evaluate the quality of their performance.

Cognitive—Students will identify and describe characteristics of folk music and explore its connections to other musical genres.

1. There are different stories about how this song came to be, which is a characteristic of folk music. Why is this? In small groups have students speculate on their ideas.
2. What is folk music? Identify characteristics of folk music and compile a list of folk songs that students know—consider having them ask their parents or grandparents.
3. Have students discover a folk song and share it with the class, either by playing it or making a recording for the class.
4. Introduce a research component in which students examine some aspect of folk music, such as origins, types, connections to other music, or comparison of different folk songs.
5. As a class, create a timeline that depicts significant events in the evolution of folk music in America and related historical events.
6. (For advanced students) Have students select a popular song and trace it back to one of the forms of roots music (Santelli and George-Warren, 2001).

Affective—Students will explore the notion of nostalgia and discuss how it is expressed in music and other art forms.

"Amazing Grace" as a launching point, have students listen to, play, and sing the song. Ask them to inter-
～ple about the memories that song evokes, or to ask if those people have memories of other songs
 ～s. Have students discuss nostalgia.

2. Distribute the text of "Shenandoah" and have students work in small groups to analyze the different emotions found in the text. Circle the key words of the text that are most expressive. What makes it nostalgic?
3. Invite students to identify one of their favorite songs and connect it to a special memory that they have experienced.
4. Have students explore how their senses help them remember past events in their lives. Have them bring in a certain food that reminds them of a previous time in their lives and describe the memory it evokes. Explore the sense of smell in a similar way. Extend to others, such as family members, teachers, or friends (see "Assessment" below).
5. Invite students to reflect upon a time/event in their lives where a particular place—a river, lake, city, neighborhood, Grandma's house, etc.—had an emotional impact upon them and journal about it.

Assessment

One of the ways we think about assessment from a CMP perspective is before, during, and after. Gathering information before teaching the piece takes into account what it is that students need to know and be able to do. For example, the National Standards suggest that students need to "Understand music in relation to history and culture" (Consortium of National Arts Education Associations, 1994). This is an example of information gathered prior to the study of the piece. One assessment task is included for each outcome, and these tasks can be implemented at various stages of learning and rehearsing "Shenandoah."

Skill Outcome—Students perform their melodies for each other and evaluate their use of phrasing, line, and expression. Evaluations are completed through use of a written rubric.

Cognitive Outcome—Students will write an essay in which they explore the following questions: What makes this song endure? Why do so many different artists perform it? What cultural connections does it have?

Affective Outcome—Choose one of the following:

1. Have students compile a list of their favorite songs that have influenced their life so far and explain how or why.
2. Have students interview a family member about songs that hold special memories for them. What was the setting or event? What is the song? What was the event surrounding this particular memory? Arrange a display of the collected memories at a concert.

Music Selection

Why are we still holding on to this composition? What makes it worth rehearsing and teaching? The qualities and criteria included in Music Selection often mimic the analysis. Several reasons for selecting (and holding on to) "Shenandoah" are included here.

1. We begin with a beautiful song, artfully arranged for mixed choir and for concert band.
2. "Shenandoah" provides an opportunity for students to develop musical sensitivity, particularly in relation to phrasing.
3. The rich historical and cultural connections associated with "Shenandoah" allow for students to expand their understanding of the work within a broader context.
4. Good design and use of form.
5. Both compositions are technically appropriate for adolescent voices or instruments.

CONCLUSION

In this chapter we examined "Shenandoah" from a choral and an instrumental perspective. The outcomes we designed are appropriate for either setting and illustrate the fluidity of the CMP model. The strategies exemplify ways in which the creativity of the teacher comes to life, and the possibilities for strategies are limited only by the teacher's imagination. A choral teacher-conductor might prefer to include a strategy that specifically addresses breath and emphasis on text; an instrumental teacher-conductor might ask students to speculate on ways in which Ticheli conveys images (e.g., "longing-ness"). In addition, varied strategies help address the National Standards (also discussed in chapter 7). In chapter 5 we will look at ways in which the CMP model can be enacted within the daily rehearsal as well as specific ideas for transferring learning from "Shenandoah" to other works.

GOING FURTHER—QUESTIONS FOR DISCUSSION

1. What do the choral and instrumental works have in common, apart from the obvious source material?
2. What compositions can you think of that could employ some of the outcomes included for "Shenandoah"?
3. In considering your beliefs and experience as a teacher and student, what strategies can you add to the "Shenandoah" teaching plan? How would you personalize it according to your philosophy?
4. In what ways does a teaching plan like the one created for "Shenandoah" advance more holistic teaching?

4

CMP and Teachers

A teacher knows something not understood by others, presumably the students. The teacher can transform understanding, performance skills, or desired attitudes or values into pedagogical representations and actions. These are ways of talking, showing, enacting, or otherwise representing ideas so that the unknowing can come to know, those without understanding can comprehend and discern, and the unskilled can become adept. (Shulman, 1987, p. 7)

FROM THE TEACHER'S POINT OF VIEW

In this chapter, we talk about what Comprehensive Musicianship through Performance (CMP) looks like from the point of view of the teacher. We begin with the teacher because it is the teacher who has a vision for the ensemble—what students need to know and be able to do, what repertoire will lead to meaningful musical experiences, and how to organize teaching and learning. A teacher with a vision toward performing with understanding will approach planning differently than a teacher with a view limited to musical performance. Teachers come to CMP with a vision toward providing a deeper musical experience for students. They not only value a high level of musical performance, but they want more—they want their students to know how a piece came to be, how it is constructed, its distinct components, and its potential for facilitating comprehensive music learning.

Also included in this chapter is a discussion of the ways CMP functions as a model for professional development for teachers at varying stages of their careers. At different phases of their careers, teachers look at CMP differently. Looking at the various stages of career development will help illuminate teacher knowledge for the preservice, novice, and veteran music educators as well as those involved in teacher education. How does CMP promote teacher cognition? In what ways does it transform the teacher and his or her practice? What is the role of experience in this process? A discussion of these questions will be useful in unpacking the many and varied layers of CMP as it relates to teacher knowledge for teachers at various stages of their careers.

TEACHER KNOWLEDGE—AN OVERVIEW

In 1985, Lee Shulman, as president of the American Educational Research Association, addressed that organization. His address, titled "Those Who Understand: Knowledge Growth and Teaching," was subsequently published in 1986 (Shulman, 1986). Shulman charged that the behavioral (process-product) view of teaching as a merely observable theory was insufficient, and that what teachers knew was just as important as what they did. Shulman introduced a theory of teacher knowledge that reflected the complexities of teachers' work, outlining several types of knowledge evidenced by practicing teachers. This seminal work has direct relevance to music teachers, and the descriptions of teacher knowledge in the next few pages include applications to the music classroom to help illustrate those connections.

Of the seven categories presented by Shulman, four categories consistently appear in some form in various studies related to teacher knowledge and music education in particular. Content knowledge includes what teachers know about a subject area, including the major facts and concepts within a field and the relationships among them. In music education, this would include general knowledge about music such as history, theory, and performance practice.

Curricular knowledge is concerned with the full range of programs designed for the teaching of particular subjects and topics as well as instructional materials related to those programs. The teacher draws upon this knowledge according to the specifics of his or her teaching/learning context. In music education, this would include categories such as repertoire selection and methods.

General pedagogical knowledge includes skills, beliefs, and knowledge regarding learners and learning, such as general principles of instruction. These include academic learning time, classroom management, and knowledge and beliefs about the goals and purposes of education. This is the most general category of teacher knowledge and transcends specializations of subject and grade level.

Among the various categories of teacher knowledge, pedagogical content knowledge is of particular significance because it addresses specifically the distinctive bodies of knowledge necessary for teaching in a discipline. This type of knowledge often parallels subject matter or content knowledge. For example, the process of planning a rehearsal calls upon knowledge of content (music) and pedagogical knowledge (appropriateness of repertoire, strategies, and objectives). The concept of pedagogical content knowledge comprises a major part of Shulman's work and is the aspect of his work that has received the most attention in music education. It goes beyond knowledge of subject matter and includes an understanding of the most useful ways of making specific topics easy or difficult, as well as an understanding of the most useful ways of representing and formulating instruction so as to make content comprehensible to others.

Many others have contributed to the body of research on teacher knowledge, including Connelly and Clandinin (1988); Grossman (1990); and Gudmundsdottir (1991). Each explored teacher knowledge in a slightly different way. Their work has a particular affinity to CMP and teachers. Connelly and Clandinin introduced a form of teacher knowledge that they called personal practical knowledge:

> Personal practical knowledge is in the teacher's past experience, in the teacher's present mind and body, and in the future plans and actions. Personal practical knowledge is found in the teacher's practice. It is, for any one teacher, a particular way of reconstructing the past and the intentions of the future to deal with the exigencies of a present situation. (1988, p. 25)

At its essence personal practical knowledge resides in the teacher's knowledge of a classroom, and this knowledge is particular to each individual teacher. It is manifested in the way the teacher approaches the many facets of teaching, including decisions about curriculum. A music teacher, for example, makes decisions about curriculum not only from one performance to the next, but over multiple years. This may include repertoire selection as well as thematic units of study.

The introduction of pedagogical content knowledge, in particular, stands out as a contribution that helped researchers as well as educators understand the importance of the teacher's understanding of various aspects of teaching. The emphasis on teacher knowledge further underscores and continues to mark the many ways of looking at the complexities of teaching rather than the previous, one-size-fits-all ways of thinking about teaching articulated by Leglar and Collay (2002). The CMP model encourages a broad range of thinking about teaching and learning, congruent with the many dimensions of teacher knowledge.

CMP VIEWED THROUGH A LENS OF TEACHER KNOWLEDGE

Repertoire Matters

One of the staples of the methods in undergraduate teacher education is the construction of a repertoire list. This is an exercise designed to help music education students gain familiarity with a corpus of repertoire for their future classroom. Typically, these lists include a variety of composers, grade levels, and styles. A comprehensive view of repertoire would also include outcomes or descriptions of what a particular piece teaches. For example, a student in a choral methods course may include "Ave Verum Corpus" on his list because it was composed by Mozart, and studying this piece will help students gain proficiency in singing espressivo. This kind of repertoire list is a useful place for young teachers to begin to know the repertoire; in fact, this is more than just another homework assignment; this is an exercise in personal practical knowledge.

Over time, these lists grow into working documents and libraries and files—a living resource sort of like sourdough ~er—you have to feed it to keep it going. Veteran teachers have amassed a knowledge of repertoire that allows ~uickly cull through catalogs, websites, and library files and select music that fits. One of the most effective ~ novice music teacher in this journey is to talk with veteran teachers and colleagues who are well ~rtoire. Personal practical knowledge permeates all that teachers do and, according to Connelly ~rder to understand teaching, it is necessary to understand the complex environment in which it exists for the individual teacher. An evolving repertoire list provides an example for the teacher-conductor throughout his or her career.

Contextual Matters

Grossman (1990) examined pedagogical content knowledge and emphasized the contextual aspect of what teachers know. When music teachers select repertoire, for example, they need to understand the particular local community and culture in which they work. Snow and Apfelstadt (2002) describe this contextual knowledge in relation to the choral setting; these assertions can be transferred to the instrumental setting as well. For example, teachers need to know the technical capabilities of their students—in a choral classroom this could involve knowledge of the changing voice. In a string orchestra this could be exemplified in specific bowing techniques.

Erin is a middle school band director. As a college student, she enjoyed performing the works of Grainger. Now that she is teaching middle school, Grainger's music is largely out of reach for her students. Instead, she has selected "Londonderry Air," arranged by John Kinyon (1990), for her students as a way to explore something that, while not at the level of Grainger, contains the same tune as his masterwork, "Irish Tune from County Derry" (Grainger, 1918). Kinyon's arrangement of the same tune, "Danny Boy," will be, in Erin's mind, a challenge with great potential for comprehensive music learning.

As she sets out to construct a CMP teaching plan, Erin crafts outcomes as she analyzes the work: students will perform with smooth technique and phrasing . . . students will identify characteristics of folk music . . . students will explore musical elements that contribute to a meaningful performance. From these broad outcomes, strategies begin to emerge. One of the ways Erin goes about this is to brainstorm several possibilities and to stretch herself as a teacher at the same time. Not always comfortable in the kinesthetic realm, for example, Erin knows kinesthetic strategies can be effective with her young band students—so she makes sure to address that in her collection of strategies. In the case of "Londonderry Air" this could include having students use their arms to show the melodic contour. Erin likes to have at least five strategies for each outcome—of those, she may not execute all, but she has a choice as she implements her teaching plan. Selected strategies may also serve as assessment tasks. For example, Erin could use a Venn[1] diagram to compare the Grainger and the Kinyon works.

The compositions that we teach may not be at the level of masterwork in the sense of Grainger's "Irish Tune," but they have the potential to inspire our students toward meaningful and lasting musical experiences. Younger students may not have the developmental sophistication to grasp the complexities of Grainger, but they do have the capacity to understand something challenging and meaningful. As a veteran teacher, Erin has the knowledge to realize what is possible and to bring something like a masterwork within her students' reach. This illustrates the teacher's personal practical knowledge and her knowledge of her students enacted in the planning process.

A Fluid Model

One way to approach the CMP model is to begin with analysis, and this can be a logical starting point as it often inspires outcomes. However, it is also possible to begin the work at another point of the model, such as strategies or outcomes. For example, I pick up a score to a new work by Timothy Broege, "Jody" (1999). Through experience I know Broege has a reputation for writing high-quality music for concert band, and I know that this piece is based on a prison work song in a minor pentatonic tonality, which intrigues me. As I page through the score, I make a list of strategies: explore call and response; compositional devices including fragmentation, diminution, repetition, augmentation; traditions of African-American music and work songs—the list goes on and on. After a few hours my list numbers well beyond thirty items. I then group the items according to skill, knowledge, and affective outcome possibilities. This process is not linear; rather, I am performing a cursory analysis that helps me brainstorm strategies that I group into three categories of outcomes.

With each look through the score my analysis deepens, and the composer's notes are rich with detail. Broege states, "Less experienced players should be encouraged to leave behind their expressive inhibitions and enter wholeheartedly into the piece. The world of Jody does not consist of sweetness, triviality, and consumerism. With considerable assistance from the performers, this music has a chance of bearing witness to some of the bad things which a just society may eventually overcome" (1999).

My excitement for teaching this work grows along with my list of strategies. I do, however, have a certain amount of trepidation and uncertainty, given the heaviness (as expressed by the composer) and musical challenges (slow, primarily soft dynamics) of this work. On the one hand, it will be challenging to inspire students to want to play something so musically demanding in its subtlety; on the other hand, "Jody" presents an ideal opportunity to take on some difficult issues, musically and culturally. But will the students get it? Will they like the piece?

As we rehearse "Jody" over many weeks, a student approaches me one day and asks if we can play it on a particular day. "Why?" I ask. "I love that piece," she replies. "What do you love about it?" I probe. "I don't know, I just really like it." That is enough for me to feel that I am on to something with my long list of strategies and passion for the piece. While unable to locate the specific words, this student has brought to the fore her own feelingful response to "Jody"; this provides affirmation and assurance to me. My choice to begin the work with strategies has enabled me to explore creative ideas for teaching "Jody" comprehensively. Creativity was also extended to the students, as they completed an assignment called the *Jody Connections Assignment*. After learning about the origins of the work, students were invited to complete a research project or original artwork related to an aspect of "Jody." Some students wrote poetry, others created drawings (both abstract and realistic), still others contributed research projects. In spite of my experience and knowledge, though, the affirmation from this student is frosting on the cake.

A Dynamic Model

Narratives of teachers' experience with CMP has demonstrated how it takes shape according to the teacher's knowledge and experience. Evelyn, a veteran middle school orchestra teacher-conductor, discussed her teaching and outcomes for a composition her students were studying. She explained that even though she starts with outcomes written on paper, these outcomes may be altered during the teaching process. Evelyn described how syncopation was the primary focus of study in an interview that took place in the third week of working on that piece. Her second outcome addressed form, and helping students understand this particular musical element.

> *Evelyn:* I'm not even close to the second outcome, the one about form . . . I'm not clear on that yet . . . maybe my outcome isn't very clear—maybe I don't really know what I want them to get from it except to see that the piece has form. This is typically how I deal with a CMP plan. In the perfect world, you would write your CMP plan: outcome, outcome, outcome, strategy, strategy, strategy, and you would select from those as you teach the piece.
>
> *Laura:* So the plan is constructed before teaching the piece?
>
> *Evelyn:* Yes, that's the perfect world. I can't do it that way. I feel like I need to go back and revisit it every time. My plan develops as I teach the piece.

In this excerpt Evelyn has described the way in which her CMP teaching plan evolves as she is engaged in the teaching process, demonstrating the experiential dimensions of personal practical knowledge (Connelly & Clandinin, 1988). It also reveals her knowledge of an idealized form of planning and the way she has personalized the process to fit her needs and interests. While she begins instruction with a general idea of the purposes for studying a particular piece, she continually revises her teaching in relation to her knowledge of students, curriculum, and educational contexts, which illustrates pedagogical content knowledge.

Teacher knowledge consists of many different types of cognition that intersect (Connelly & Clandinin, 1988; Grossman, 1990; Shulman, 1986, 1987). In contrast to an emphasis on teacher characteristics, the assumption in teacher knowledge research is that the most important area to study is what teachers know and the ways this knowledge is manifested in teaching. Within music education, findings about teacher knowledge indicate that it is individually constructed, informed by personal history, and experience based. CMP is a model for curriculum, instruction, and assessment; therefore, it is dependent upon particular kinds of teacher cognition for its successful implementation.

THE DIFFERENT PHASES OF A TEACHING LIFE AND CMP—STORIES FROM THE FIELD

CMP and Preservice Music Educators

One form of dissemination of CMP takes place in undergraduate methods classes. Persons preparing to enter the classroom participate in education that is musically rigorous from the standpoint of applied lessons, ensembles, and theory and history. They also take techniques and methods courses specific to music teaching and learning as well as several courses that satisfy state licensure requirements. Within the methods courses, it is not unusual for undergraduate students ̀ ᴠe some exposure to comprehensive musicianship—the nature of that exposure is unknown, resulting in an incom-
ᵉ of methods courses and their inclusion of comprehensive musicianship in general or CMP in particular.
ⁿerience for students preparing to enter the profession? In what ways does their thinking about CMP
ᴵ°rgraduate experience? One student, Richard, recalled his first experience with CMP as "think-
ᵉned up the world that there is a way to teach music out there that is not just kill and

drill." As he went through the process of writing CMP teaching plans, Richard described "hours and hours of daunting work . . . plowing through the score, looking up information . . . it was nuts how much work went into writing one lesson plan."

The process of writing the teaching plan organized his thoughts and provided a road map for teaching his selected piece. He knew more about the piece and had direction in relation to what he should teach with his selected piece. "It made my time on the podium more enjoyable and much less terrifying." As a student teacher, Richard had a few opportunities to road test his teaching plans, both at the high school and middle school levels. He concluded, "Even if I do not accomplish every single one of my outcomes, at least writing the plan gives me a guide on what I need to think about in the music, and in turn what I need to get my students thinking about. Even if I use concepts that CMP sets forth and don't use the lesson plan, at least I know more about the music to make it better for my students." Richard has demonstrated an evolution in his thinking and experience in relation to CMP, and this has left a lasting impression.

As undergraduate students in methods courses, students can become familiar with CMP and create their own teaching plans. With increasing emphasis on fieldwork in public schools, as a component of teacher preparation those teaching plans can be implemented on a limited scale in practicum or lab sessions. The student teaching experience, then, provides an in-depth opportunity to continue trying out these ideas as they navigate a balance between monitoring and adjusting the written plan and responding to immediate needs that arise as the rehearsal unfolds (Snow & Apfelstadt, 2002). Placing student teachers with cooperating teachers who value CMP is not only helpful but critical to connecting the work of the methods classes with the reality of school ensembles.

Kari grew up in a CMP classroom as a middle school student and had exposure to CMP as an undergraduate music education student. She reflected on her middle school band experience, describing it as "inspiring and gratifying." During student teaching Kari was free to integrate any strategies she wanted to, but this was not in line with the established routine, and her attempts were a "great struggle." In Kari's words, "The culture of the classroom is hard to impact when you are the one in charge, much less a short-term student teacher." Despite this, she did continue to attempt various CMP teaching plans with varying levels of success. The anecdotes of Richard and Kari illustrate their developing knowledge base.

CMP and Novice Music Educators

An example of the shift that comes with experience was provided by Maria, a novice orchestra teacher, as she described her desire to delve more deeply into the music and the impact on students. "My level of understanding of just how powerful this model can be increased as I really began to implement CMP plans and make CMP a part of my daily teaching." According to Maria, students learn more and perform at a higher level on these compositions.

An example of a teacher's desire to delve more deeply into the music and the impact upon her students was described by Michelle, a novice choral music teacher. "My level of understanding of just how powerful this model can be increased as I began to really implement CMP plans and make it a part of my daily teaching." The pieces for which Michelle writes teaching plans are, in her words, "always the students' favorite." According to Michelle, students learn more and perform at a higher level on these compositions. Over time, she felt she became more adept at not only being better able to diagnose and solve musical problems in rehearsal, but also to incorporate comprehensive musicianship *through* the performance of her choral ensembles.

With experience, teachers become more efficient in their work and more confident in their abilities. This can be difficult for student teachers and novice teachers to deal with. It's like teaching a piece for the second time. The teacher feels more confident and has more knowledge and experience of what makes the music come alive. This is evident in a vignette from Mr. Gabriel's orchestra rehearsal and discussed in the next section.

CMP and Veteran Music Educators

In the opening vignettes of chapter 1, we saw several examples of how Mr. Gabriel applies the CMP model and teaching plan he created for *Battalia*; these examples also illustrate his pedagogical knowledge. The selected excerpts show many creative strategies that engage the students while allowing the teacher to exercise his creative teaching ideas. One compelling example took place during a rehearsal when students were writing their letter home as part of their study of the emotions of war. Mr. Gabriel described the setting: "The room was very still; it was almost like there was an intense silence. The students were not looking at one another or looking to see what anybody else wrote. They were immersed in their own thoughts." I asked Mr. Gabriel, "How did you instruct the students that the writing was over and you were going to play the piece?"

"I observed the students writing, and when I felt like about 80 to 90 percent of them looked like they were finished, I said there would be two more minutes of writing time and they should finish their thoughts. After two minutes I said that even if you were not done writing, we would play the movement. And I spoke in a very soft tone so as to not disturb the environment that had been created when students were writing their letters." We can imagine the feeling of this room during this experience—and the way this experience brought the students closer to the music they were studying.

The body of Mr. Gabriel's knowledge of his students and his subject, in combination with his experience, provide a powerful learning experience for all. As a teacher with several years of experience, Mr. Gabriel has amassed a body of knowledge as described in the work of Shulman, Clandinin, Connelly, and others. Over time, his expertise in using CMP facilitates a seamless experience for students in which the letter-writing episode takes place as something that is just as important as tuning.

CMP AS A MODEL FOR PROFESSIONAL DEVELOPMENT

Like other pedagogical models (such as Kodaly, Orff-Schulwerk, and Suzuki), there are several avenues for sharing the CMP model with teachers, including workshops and conference presentations. The primary vehicle for disseminating the CMP model, particularly in relation to professional development, is through the annual summer workshops. These week-long workshops are held in various locations and are intended to immerse participants in study and application of the CMP model. Members of the CMP Project serve as workshop staff, providing instruction at sessions and using their own teaching plans as exemplars for attendees. CMP Project members draw upon their own classrooms as they guide other teachers in the application of the model in the ensemble setting.

Teachers who attend the workshop apply the planning process to compositions they intend to present to their students as they observe demonstration rehearsals, attend sessions in which each point of the model is presented, and work in small groups on their individual projects. The workshop also includes presentations of current topics in music education, such as portfolio assessment, use of technology, and standards-based curricula. Many of these materials have been included in *Shaping Sound Musicians* (O'Toole, 2003). For those less familiar with CMP, the learning curve can be steep. Small breakout groups facilitated by a CMP committee member provide a nurturing space in which to clarify material, challenge one another, and ask questions on any number of topics, whether related to CMP specifically or tangentially. The breakout groups help facilitate understanding on the part of the teachers attending the workshop, sort of like a study group one might have in a college class.

Teachers who participate in other varieties of professional development presentations are at various positions along the continuum of their teaching careers. Consequently, they take away different things from their experience. Young teachers may be motivated to attend a workshop because they may have had some exposure to CMP but seek a more detailed experience. Following their initial workshop, novice teachers are encouraged to implement one teaching plan in the upcoming school year. The largest number of teachers attending the CMP workshop is veteran teachers, many of whom attend the workshop multiple times. Many of the veteran teachers describe a desire to be more planful; improve their teaching; and reflect on their personal beliefs about teaching and learning. Like teachers everywhere, they are motivated to attend this workshop because they seek to improve their teaching, and to teach more in-depth.

What happens when these teachers return to their school? How do they move forward or sustain their vision of performing with understanding when faced with the reality of life in the school? These are important questions to ask in relation to understanding the impact of CMP on teachers and students. Many veteran teachers comment that they adopt a CMP approach in general to their teaching and that they think in a more comprehensive manner and eventually apply aspects of CMP to all the pieces they are teaching. It is also not uncommon for teachers to return to the workshop multiple times.

INTENTION

The glue that binds this work together, regardless of years of teaching experience, is *intention*—a universal component of effective teaching in many contexts. To illustrate, I draw upon an example from the yoga studio. I've studied yoga with Tina for a little over three years. I vividly recall my first class: we dutifully laid out our mats and props, a few of us chatted softly. The teacher gently began by inviting us to lie down for the first portion of the class, savasana (in a rehearsal, the parallel would be warming up). During savasana, Tina shared a poem, a literary example of mindfulness, and followed with our intention for this practice. She did not refer to it as *her* intention, but one shared by all—it was *our* intention. After a series of poses on the earth, hand and knees, standing, and one or two especially challenging poses, we returned to the earth for meditation. We were reminded of the poem and of our intention for this practice. After several minutes of silence the sound of the bell reawakened us and we prepared to reenter the world outside. The architecture of Tina's yoga class included components shared by good teachers, shaped by intention, which guided our experience.

The origins and organizing principles of the CMP model depend upon the teacher, who serves as the catalyst for implementing instruction. The teacher selects repertoire, analyzes it, and plans instructional activities. The teacher constructs outcomes and related strategies with specific intentions and learning goals; this learning is measured through planned assessments. The merging of teacher knowledge, in its many forms, and CMP takes place through various forms of dissemination.

CONCLUSION

How do CMP and the teacher fit together, and what is the result? With its open framework, CMP does two important things: like many structures, it provides the outer walls; it also calls for the teacher to utilize her or his creativity, passions, and most importantly, vision.

Gudmundsdottir (1991) found that teachers constructed a pedagogical model that was grounded in his or her pedagogical content knowledge. While each model was distinctive, they shared an important element: "They are the teachers' homemade maps of the discipline they teach and they show how the teachers feel the discipline should be sequenced for pedagogical purposes" (p. 293). A planning framework such as the CMP model is well suited to adaptation and modification by the individual teacher. One teacher may select repertoire that challenges the students technically and emotionally, thereby improving the students' technical abilities through the repertoire. Another teacher may develop creative exercises that will help students gain skills that will lead them to the study of more advanced repertoire. The idea of personalizing a model in a way that is in alignment with the teacher's philosophy is very much a part of the construction and implementation of the CMP teaching plan, and one of its enduring features.

Much of what teachers learn about teaching as well as what it means to teach is learned through being a teacher. This includes learning from the process of teaching, learning from students, learning from other teachers, and learning from the subject matter. Ultimately, what Clandinin and Connelly refer to as narratives of experience of teachers and students "interweave and mingle such that both are educated" (1988, p. 197). CMP invites the teacher to make choices and decisions about instruction, thereby activating the particular blend of the teacher's knowledge.

GOING FURTHER—QUESTIONS FOR DISCUSSION

1. In what ways does *performing with understanding* influence how music repertoire is taught by the teacher?
2. How might understanding gained through a CMP approach help or hinder the musical performance of a piece?
3. In what ways might an inservice situated in CMP influence professional development for new teachers and for veteran teachers? What would be the same? What would be different?
4. Select a musical concept and develop five different ways for a teacher to present this concept in a band, choir, or orchestra setting.
5. What considerations does a music teacher need to make in selecting repertoire for a concert cycle, for the school year, and for multiple years?

NOTE

1. Venn diagram is an analysis tool initially referenced in chapter 1. Its intersecting circles can be configured in many ways as a means for comparing and contrasting musical works.

5

Enacting the Teaching Plan

I think a lot about how much time I have to prepare the music, which limits the depth of comprehensive learning that I feel I can attempt . . . performing at a high musical level is very important to the students' musical experience. Teaching in a comprehensive way, I believe, leads to a higher level of performance and does not take away from the performance level if the outcomes and strategies are thoughtfully crafted from the music being studied.

—Mr. Gabriel, high school orchestra teacher-conductor

TAKING "SHENANDOAH" INTO THE CLASSROOM

The process of analysis and creating the Comprehensive Musicianship through Performance (CMP) teaching plan is an exercise in planning instruction and has been detailed in previous chapters. The investment of planning, in particular, is essential to ensure a quality performance and comprehensive learning.

One of the most personally charged issues in examining the CMP music experience is the place (classroom) and perspective and work of the teacher. In the CMP practice,[1] the teacher is responsible for planning instruction. This goes well beyond rehearsal planning and error detection and includes long-term goals as well as organizing thematic units, which may or may not form the focus of a concert. In this chapter we will explore how the teaching plan comes to life in the rehearsal, from introducing a composition to rehearsing it over time, particularly in light of the many and varied expectations in addition to preparing a single work. We will also look at concert programming and the ways in which a single CMP teaching plan can influence the choice of other repertoire and reinforce similar outcomes. This chapter brings together our overview of CMP, application to "Shenandoah", and distinct knowledge of the teacher-conductor.

INTRODUCING THE PIECE

The way we introduce students to a new piece of music provides a rich opportunity for comprehensive musicianship. Wiggins (2001) describes this as "opening a doorway," suggesting new discoveries and multiple possibilities from the beginning. The introduction of a new piece can create immediate interest on the part of the students and jumpstart the learning process. This can greatly influence how students react during the initial stages of learning a new piece and will likely form a lasting impression. In chapter 1 we read about the way Mr. Gabriel introduced *Battalia*, asking students to play scales in multiple keys at the same time, introducing the concept of dissonance, and then to take out the piece they thought contained dissonance. These strategies pique student interest as they prepare to sight read *Battalia*, demonstrating how a teacher-conductor can highlight its distinct features to immediately engage students.

A high school choral teacher, Mary, opens the doorway on a new piece for her students by first providing the text to "A Quiet Moment," by Jennifer Higdon (1999). She asks students, "If you were the composer, how would you set the text?" They list responses on a board for all to see: slow tempo, smooth and flowing, stepwise, big intervals, dissonant, polyphonic, consonant, homophonic, are among the responses. Next, the students are given a copy of the music and analyze the work using a study sheet prepared by their teacher. The teacher's intention is for students to analyze the work and to see what they can discover about a piece without even hearing it. Mary made it possible for students to think as musicians, using their imagination and existing knowledge to reach more deeply into the work they were studying.

Returning briefly to our work with "Shenandoah," we can apply the notion of "doorway in" through an affective strategy included under the affective outcome of that teaching plan: Have students reflect upon a time/event in their lives where a particular place—a river, lake, city, neighborhood, or Grandma's house—had an emotional impact upon them and reflect on it. This could be included as a journal activity or class discussion before the piece is handed out as a way to spark a level of emotion or nostalgia that is also part of the planned study of "Shenandoah" at the introductory phase.

INFUSING THE TEACHING PLAN INTO THE REHEARSAL—FROM PLANNING TO IMPLEMENTATION

Within the regular rehearsal routine, how does CMP fit? We begin this discussion by examining some of the standard components of the ensemble rehearsal. The teacher-conductor typically generates a list of things that need attention (most often "fixing"), determines an order for the work, and proceeds through the list in an effort to make forward progress. Several authors have delineated various planning processes for the rehearsal (Colwell & Hewitt, 2011; Cooper, 2004; Hylton, 1995; Kohut, 1996; Labuta, 1997). Among the standard components of the rehearsal are warm-ups, announcements, perhaps some technical exercises and repertoire. The amount of repertoire varies according to factors such as approaching concert dates, rehearsal length and frequency, and age or level of students. Also related to the repertoire portion is the level of progress of the particular ensemble on individual compositions. Sometimes teacher-conductors will include ear training, theory exercises, or listening activities within the rehearsal period and have been shown to improve student behavior and attention to both tasks and the teacher (Cox, 1989; Witt, 1986). The process of planning in the ensemble setting includes the regular rehearsal period (daily, weekly, or a variation thereof) as well as a longer view, often a concert cycle of six to eight weeks.

The rehearsal planning process can vary greatly from one teacher to the next. For some, rehearsal planning includes selecting scores from among those in the folder minutes before the rehearsal begins. Others may spend hours studying the intricacies of a composition, analyzing and marking a score to internalize a work. Some teacher-conductors will make a list of potential "trouble spots," such as highly technical passages or those with complicated harmonies.

We hope that those teacher-conductors keep mindful of the *students* in the ensembles as well, planning ways to involve the students in helping to meet challenges in the music. The planning process is distinct to the individual teacher-conductor, and his or her vision for the ensemble. How then, does the CMP teaching plan become part of the rehearsal? How does it blend in among the typical rehearsal procedures and lead to musical understanding without compromising high standards of musical performance?

Connecting Warm-Ups to the Repertoire

One effective way to infuse a CMP teaching plan into a rehearsal is to connect rehearsal warm-ups and skill development related to a specific piece. For example, our "Shenandoah" teaching plan includes the following skill outcome: Students will perform with smooth and expressive phrasing. An effective warm-up strategy, then, could be to play or sing other folk song melodies with extended legato lines in unison. This is an efficient way of blending the critical opening portion with musical learning that builds a deeper experience. Warm-ups can also be used to improve students' lasting skills related to the pieces being studied. This could include ear training or recognizing chord progressions in the score.

The Rehearsal

It may not be practical to devote an entire rehearsal to a single piece in the school setting, given the multiple tasks that need tending to and being mindful of limitations such as time as well as the age level of the students. Middle school students typically have a shorter attention span than high school students, for example. Transposing the detailed CMP plan for implementation into the regular rehearsal involves selecting smaller components, such as selected strategies or assessment tasks, and focusing on a single outcome. Table 5.1 includes a copy of a daily rehearsal plan that could be useful for day-to-day implementation of a CMP teaching plan.

Labuta provides another example of a daily rehearsal plan and ways it can be adapted to advance comprehensive musicianship by giving careful consideration to the warm-ups and technical drill rehearsal segments in addition to

Table 5.1. Daily Rehearsal Plan

Daily Rehearsal Plan
Ensemble/Context:
Date:
Repertoire:
Goals for this piece (state briefly): Skill Knowledge Affective
Goal for today:
Selected strategies (steps for achieving today's goal). Include warm-ups that are instructional and related to outcome when appropriate. 1. 2. 3. 4. 5.
Assessment of today's teaching/learning:
Assignment:
Announcements:
Reminders for self:
What's next?

careful rehearsal of selected repertoire (1997). Table 5.2 depicts the events of a high school rehearsal observed by the author as a third example of infusing CMP into the rehearsal.

As we recall the anecdotes of the first chapter, students were reminded to make corrections in counting, bowing, and intonation; they were also asked many, many questions in the quest to understand and explore why the composer wrote *Battalia* as he did. Questions such as, "What do you think this is about? Why do you think Biber did this? How did he do that?" are used in an ongoing effort to invite students to ponder, to interpret, and to think deeply about the music they are studying. They are useful prompts in our discussion of bringing CMP into the rehearsal.

Contingencies

Unplanned events and occurrences are part of most rehearsals. This can range from testing to fire drills to student absences to any number of contingencies that comprise the teaching day. The convergence of factors upon the rehearsal, planned or otherwise, calls for striking some kind of balance, given the unknown and unexpected.

Two teachers, one at the middle school level and one at the high school level, talked about how, as their teaching plans were implemented, each of the plans were met with unexpected events. Ray, a high school teacher, indicated that interruptions were frequent. "Well, as plans go, there is always the unexpected. We had a shortened class period today and all of the junior class had PSAT[2] testing today." While it was clear that Ray planned rehearsals, it was also clear that he recognized that disruptions frequently occurred. He seemed to have reconciled this reality with his desire for a high-level musical performance and desire to implement CMP, and modified his plans as necessary. Ray described the circumstances that caused him to reevaluate a programming decision:

We have two rehearsals this week, both without the sophomores due to state testing. I lose Friday's rehearsal because of parent-teacher conferences. That leaves me with one remaining rehearsal next Tuesday—the day of the concert. With that said, I have decided to program one less movement of (Vaughan Williams') *English Folk Song Suite*. I shared this programming change with the students today and they fully supported the change in programming.

Table 5.2.   High School Choral Rehearsal

Length (approximate)	Composition	Activities
2-3 minutes	Warm-ups	Stretching
10 minutes	*Salmo 150* Emani Aguilar (1993)	Technical work on rhythm, diction, and tone in selected measures. Sing through the piece from the beginning.
20 minutes	*A Quiet Moment* Jennifer Higdon (1999)	Students take out their journal folders and a worksheet. They compare their ideas for setting a particular text to music with the published score of that text and work independently, analyzing the score. Students share responses, Next, they examine their individual part (SATB) to rate the level of difficulty of their part, using a scale of 1-10.
10 minutes	*Can You Hear?* Jim Papoulis (2004)	Solfege review, then text, in selected sections.

Ray did not feel that his students would be prepared to perform the entire *English Folk Song Suite* at the concert, so he chose to make an adjustment to the program. He discussed this with his students and indicated they understood and accepted his decision (Sindberg, 2006).

The CMP model is a framework, and in the process of teaching, the framework and teaching plan are altered as seen as necessary by the teacher and the particularities of his or her classroom on any given day.

TOWARD MUSICAL UNDERSTANDING

Rehearsals represent the steps we take along the way to understanding the music we perform. Enacting the teacher's vision takes place over time, through those steps. Another component of infusing CMP into the ensemble setting, then, has to do with enacting the teacher's vision over time—whether a single school year or multiple years, such as middle school or high school. In the case of some districts, that span could encompass middle school and high school.

The notion of enactment over time is directly related to long-term outcomes. These may be linked to repertoire, performance expectations, national or state standards, or local school district initiatives. The process of enactment over time contributes to musical understanding in the ensemble setting. Reimer (2000) posits the national standards as a mechanism designed to broaden musical understandings "so as to include all major dimensions of music as a human endeavor" (p. 23).

Determining several long-term goals related to musical understanding can be an effective way to incorporate CMP into the ensemble. An example of a long-term goal applicable over a school year could be, students will develop lasting skills that enable them to recognize balance in an ensemble. An example of a goal that could endure over multiple years (program goal) could be, students will be able to identify distinct musical styles and periods and describe characteristics of each. These goals can be addressed within individual compositions (short term) as well as the long-term outcomes.

CMP AND CONCERT PROGRAMMING

Concert programming provides another opportunity to incorporate CMP with an eye toward a longer view of the musical experience in the ensemble setting that can, in turn, serve as an educational tool in a broader context. This is especially useful in the realm of concert programming. The idea of concerts that teach has been addressed by O'Toole (2003) and Sindberg (1998). Concerts that teach include sharing what students have learned about the repertoire they have prepared with the audience. Not only can this contribute to advocacy, perhaps more important is the way in which concerts and concert programming can educate the audience, particularly about the learning that has taken place in the ensemble. We will consider one approach to concert programming using the lens of CMP. The steps involved can be readily applied in virtually any ensemble setting.

We begin with "Shenandoah" at the center. Next, we brainstorm all topics that come to mind in relation to "Shenandoah." These could include folk song, images and music, American music, use of motives, or music of Frank Ticheli. One of those components could inspire several related pieces, forming a thematic unit of study similar to that described by Garofalo (1983). For example, many fine works have been written for choral and instrumental ensembles that use folk music as source material. A concert of folk music has rich potential, examples of which are included in sources described earlier. Figure 5.1 provides an illustration of an approach to concert programming centered on a comprehensive study of "Shenandoah."

EXCELLENCE IN PERFORMANCE AND MUSICAL UNDERSTANDING

A teacher-conductor new to CMP may fear a loss of high performance standards. This is not a necessary by-product; in fact, the examples included throughout this book clearly demonstrate a balance of both excellence in musical performance and musical understanding, and this is reinforced by several research studies done on comprehensive musicianship in the ensemble setting (Garofalo & Whaley, 1979; Sherburn, 1984; Swearingen, 1993). Kennell re-inforces the importance of musicianship and performance skills, arguing that the development of musicianship is a "means for attaining and sustaining excellence in performance" (2002, p. 196). Performance and understanding are not mutually exclusive in the CMP practice, as the examples demonstrate. A novice teacher, Peter, describes his experience incorporating CMP into his teaching:

> The biggest challenge I had was in basic implementation of a plan. I found that writing CMP plans came rather easy to me. However, my understanding of what went into teaching band was still emerging, and it became difficult to me to anticipate what would really need to be addressed. Also, in two of my three positions I began with a relatively low-functioning ensemble. Whether it was good or not, I modified my plans to include more skill-based outcomes to address the performance proficiency of the groups. I have found that as my management skills have improved, so has my ability to question students' understandings in the learning process, stimulate discussion, and address some of the "total musical" concepts that I may be interested in addressing through a CMP plan. Writing a CMP has never been the issue, but the level to which I can implement with success can still be improved.

It's not unusual for a teacher to struggle with enacting a CMP teaching plan on a regular basis, given the myriad demands placed upon teacher, students, and program. In the case of Peter, we see another example of the ongoing evolution of the teacher's CMP practice through his efforts to contribute to the intellectual and aesthetic development of the students.

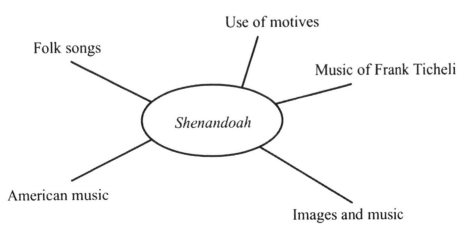

Figure 5.1. Programming Diagram

Creating and implementing a CMP teaching plan calls upon the teacher-conductor to reflect on earlier experiences that led him or her to become a teacher; often these experiences are life changing and passion filled, and he or she uses those powerful events to motivate students to engage fully in the musical experience in band, choir, and orchestra (O'Toole, 2003). O'Toole includes several ideas for taking the first steps for teacher-conductors new to CMP, including making small-scale changes in the rehearsal and taking new risks.

An example of incorporating a value of excellent performance and musical understanding comes from the classroom of Mr. Gabriel. As the orchestra reviews the first movement, playing and identifying the rhythmic motive, they are reminded to play on the string and to use the upper half of the bow. Their teacher asks, "What part of the bow should you change to for forte?" Details of bowing are crucial to the excellent performance—here we see this teacher address both performance and understanding. There is a common thread in these excerpts—a consistent attention to details of performance and excellence in performance. Standards of high musical performance are not compromised by the implementation of CMP; rather, they are enhanced.

Linking strategies and musical understanding as we enact CMP disrupts what teachers and students are accustomed to as part of the ensemble rehearsal. Teachers may view these kinds of activities as detrimental. In fact, strategies that are outside simply blowing, bowing, and striking provide views and perspectives on musical understanding that are valuable mechanisms that then allow access to the many ways students are thinking about music; they deepen student understanding.

THE STUDENTS' EXPERIENCE AS CMP IS IMPLEMENTED

While much of the discussion has been focused on the teacher—analyzing repertoire and creating a CMP teaching plan as we bring the work into the rehearsal—it is important to also keep an eye toward the students and their musical experience. With strategies designed to invite student contributions, CMP is a mechanism for fostering a student-centered classroom. Several examples were included in the opening chapter; in these examples we saw students experiment with creating unique sounds on their instruments, exploring unfamiliar harmonic devices such as polyphony, and composing a letter in which they express their thoughts and feelings about war. No longer the quietest, most orderly rehearsal room, the feel of a classroom in which students are so actively engaged has a different kind of energy.

Among the learning activities included in the study of *Battalia* was an experience in which students composed a letter to their families as if preparing to leave for war. This letter writing, however, was strategically placed in the rehearsal and made effective through previous strategies. For example, the first activity in the rehearsal was to play through the second movement, "The Profligate Society of Common Humor." Their teacher connected this movement to the music of Charles Ives, who also employed polytonality, specifically in portraying marching bands as they approached and passed by in a parade. Next, the group rehearsed the "Battle" movement. Mr. Gabriel asked students to think about how they would describe that movement and share their ideas with their stand partners. "Intense and emotional; theatrical (like a staged act of a battle); victorious" are among the student responses. Their teacher asks, "Was Biber trying to depict a battle or make fun of a battle?" He tells the students that they will discuss this and speculate on how Biber may have felt about war.

These strategies lead the group to Mr. Gabriel's next direction: "Today I would like to do the movement we haven't done yet. Which movement is that?" Students respond: "Aria." They sight read the movement, and Mr. Gabriel, ever watchful for musical details, asks the group to play again, but this time *piano*. He asks students to take out their portfolios and, without talking, describe the kind of emotion of battle Biber is trying to communicate in this movement. He also calls upon students to speculate on why the movement is called "Aria." A brief discussion follows, in which students describe fear of battle, worries about going into battle, calm before the storm, preparation, and the idea of a prayer. When he asks why the movement is called "Aria," one student says, "The soldiers are feeling alone." Following this discussion, Mr. Gabriel asks students to imagine they are being shipped to Iraq or Afghanistan, and "you are writing a letter to your family, not knowing whether or not you will come back. Write a letter to your family. We won't be sharing these." While we have read about this powerful experience in chapter 1, here we see the steps Mr. Gabriel took to lead his students to this somber moment in a carefully thought-out manner; steps that help portray one way that a CMP teaching plan is lived out among students and teacher.

How do students in a "CMP classroom" describe their experience? In a postconcert conversation, several students talked about learning *Battalia*, describing various aspects of their experience, and some of their impressions. One student commented that "The *process* of learning the piece, as well as the concert itself, was great. Singing the lullabies and discussing it, writing the letter. It really got us to open our ears and our eyes and helped us to come together and work together." Two others commented that:

> I can now apply what I learned, I think, because also last year I was in the freshman orchestra, so not with all of the upperclassmen, so now I get the other ideas of them, and not just the kids in my grade, and now I can apply what I learned in this piece to learn more about the piece, and to put more feeling into it, into *other* pieces, and I think [it was] especially cool to learn about *Battalia* because it was like a *real* story. Like it was written about something that really happened—that you could easily look up and learn about.

> I think that because the piece was maybe not as like, challenging technically as other pieces we play, I think that like, helped us, so we could not necessarily *pay* attention to the notes, but we could *pay* attention to the emotion and we could *pay* attention to everybody else, so I think that was good that the piece wasn't as demanding or challenging.

The comments of these students serve to endorse the careful attention to intention and to facilitating understanding in this classroom. A single question can often provide focus for a rehearsal that invites students to listen and think critically in relation to the music they are learning. In a middle school band rehearsal, I asked students to listen to a recording of "A Shaker Gift Song," arranged by Frank Ticheli (2004), following a brief warm-up playing patterns in 6/8. The work is based on a Shaker lullaby, "Here Take This Lovely Flower." Just prior to listening to the piece, I asked the students if anyone remembered being sung to as a small child and to describe some of those songs. Some of the students also described their experiences singing lullabies to young children. As they listened to the recording, I asked students to describe those things that made Ticheli's piece sound like a lullaby. This is reminiscent of Mr. Gabriel's inquiry of how a composer uses the tools of music to construct or portray certain kinds of effects. We shared responses and continued by playing through the piece in the style of a lullaby.

One student commented on her experience in a CMP-infused classroom, many years later and now in her own teaching practice:

> My experience with CMP as a young middle school musician brought me closer to music than I was aware of at the time. There was never a moment in band where my mind stood still, and I cannot say that about any other class. I was always wondering about music: What was my role? Who had the melody? What part of the form were we in at m. 156? Why did the composer write one particular phrase marking instead of something else? Why did I love this music?

These examples, from the voices of students, help us to see the impact of a comprehensive musicianship approach on our students. While not every student will have the same experience, and some of our students may prefer to simply "play," the notion of creating variety in regular rehearsals and its positive effects is well documented (Cox, 1989; Spradling, 1985; Witt, 1986). Kennell also talks about the importance of fostering musicianship on the part of students in ensembles and provides several questions similar to those mentioned by our student in the previous section (2002). Examples include, "Which instruments have the melody?" "From where in the melody does that accompaniment figure come?" or "Which note in the cadence sounds as if it doesn't belong?" (2002, p. 194).

INTERSECTIONS OF THE POINTS OF THE CMP MODEL—A FUNCTION OF ENACTMENT

The intersections of the CMP model reflect the way it "morphs" from a diagram delineating distinct components (analysis, assessment, music selection, outcomes, and strategies) into something that integrates those components within the rehearsal. As a teacher rehearses a piece, he or she rehearses by form rather than rehearsal letters or measure numbers: "Let's begin at the recapitulation." This is an example that shows how, in the course of a rehearsal, a teacher can assess whether the students understand the form as they participate in the analysis of the work. Differences in implementation of the CMP model are the result of the teacher's experience, beliefs, and context in which he or she teaches; teachers versed in comprehensive musicianship are also capable of modifying plans depending on the particularities of a given day.

Even with a model as elegant, integrated, and thoughtfully constructed as CMP, teachers transform the model as they enact it in their classrooms. The model is altered because some of the points may be more important to one teacher than another. For example, a teacher may place a high value on repertoire selection, or a teacher may emphasize varied strategies in pursuit of selected outcomes (Sindberg, 2006). While enacting the teaching plan, the lines of the "star" collapse on themselves, and the delineations between the points of the model become less clear. This is part of the process of working with the CMP model: it is necessary to start with a structure, but the dynamics and process of teaching result in a gestalt that is what the students see or experience. The points of the model reinforce particular components, but they are part of one huge piece.

TRANSFER REVISITED

Transfer of learning is key to the educational process, in and out of the music classroom. This was addressed in chapter 2, but our discussion here considers transfer in a broader arena. The notion that what is learned earlier will have an effect on later learning is a basic tenet of education and accepted learning theory. Jerome Bruner stated, "Learning should not only take us somewhere; it should allow us later to go further more easily" (1977, p. 17). Teachers hope that students will transfer what is learned in one piece to another piece, and it is perhaps this ubiquitous aspiration that may result in erroneous assumptions about students and their abilities to transfer learning from one context to another. Transfer is more likely to occur if it is specifically addressed through the teaching and learning process; according to Tunks (1992), transfer cannot be taken for granted.

Students may independently transfer learning from one context to another, as in the case of Maureen, who described how her part in *Folk Song Suite* had a countermelody, as did her part in a march her band was rehearsing. Another student, Melissa, drew a connection between the program outcome of excellence in her middle school band and the notion of excellence described by her dance teacher (Sindberg, 2006). In their own way, students make connections about music to other contexts in ways that make sense to them. In my own teaching practice I noticed that it was difficult for students to make connections about the music they were studying. Comparing the form of two different compositions or making connections between music they are learning in band with music they listen to outside of school are two examples I observed in my own students. Things that I assumed would transfer easily often did not without deliberate actions on my part, and even then transfer did not always occur. I realized that while some students were able to transfer learning from one piece to another, I needed to help students make connections between and among different pieces and contexts.

Teachers can facilitate transfer on the part of their students to more effectively help deepen their learning in band, choir, and orchestra. Are there ways to make transfer more intentional? What might be some examples? One of the ways in which transfer may be facilitated is to ask students a relatively simple question, such as "What makes this a good piece of music?" repeated over the course of a year, applied to multiple compositions. Over time, this question can yield responses that indicate a growing understanding of the musical elements that may not have happened without deliberate action.

Well-written outcomes can be used multiple times with different repertoire and different strategies, providing another mechanism for facilitating transfer. An example of this was shared in chapter 3, where we looked at "Shenandoah" from an instrumental and choral perspective. These outcomes could be applied to other repertoire, such as other works based on folk music, American music, and the like. In a second example, a teacher created an outcome that asked for students to be able to perform in a Baroque style. Later that year, the teacher presented a different Baroque composition and used the same outcome. The teacher found that the students were able to transfer their knowledge immediately to the second Baroque piece and sight read it in the proper style. The students in Mr. Gabriel's orchestra used their understanding of Biber and the Baroque era to more deeply understand music of that time period as well as Biber's unique compositional style.

CONCLUSION

Benner (1972) reminds us that performing groups such as band, choir, and orchestra are traditionally expected to develop performance skills; however, students in these ensembles can potentially learn more than performance skills. He suggested that a planned effort on the part of the teacher can enrich the performing experience with additional kinds of understanding, such as knowledge of history and literature. As we bring CMP into the rehearsal, we expand ideas about teaching in the ensemble and invite our students to participate more fully in the experience. The infusion of CMP into the rehearsal setting represents a shift from the traditional ensemble experience of the past and promises to stretch students and teacher-conductors in new ways; it's about reframing the rehearsal. In its application among various teachers, the CMP practice is highly individualized from teacher to teacher, which may appear paradoxical. On the one hand, this diverse way of interpreting and implementing instruction is exciting and electric; on the other hand, there is no standardized definition of the CMP practice, other than the framework of the model as enacted by the teacher. The framework delineates details regarding strategies, assessment, analysis, and outcomes—but as the teaching plans are implemented, this demarcation dissolves. The result is a musical experience that consists of performing with understanding.

GOING FURTHER—QUESTIONS FOR DISCUSSION

1. Thoughts on getting started enacting CMP into the rehearsal. What are three things you could incorporate into a rehearsal as a way to introduce CMP to your students?
2. Select a composition and devise two different strategies for introducing the work.
3. What are three barriers you can think of that would interfere with enacting a CMP teaching plan? How would you address each one?
4. Do you agree with the idea that transfer is not an automatic enterprise? How might you facilitate transfer of learning in the ensemble?
5. Select a composition that could serve as a centerpiece for a unit of study or concert and list related works and the ways they are connected, as in the "Shenandoah" concert programming example.

NOTES

1. CMP practice refers to the ways in which a teacher implements the CMP model in his or her particular ensemble setting—it is the sum of the various parts of the CMP model put into practice.
2. This refers to the Preliminary SAT/National Merit Qualifying test, a precursor to the SAT.

6

CMP and the Music Curriculum

To speak of craft is to presume a knowledge of a certain range of skills and proficiencies. It is to imagine an educated capacity to attain a desired end-in-view or to bring about a desired result. Where teachers are concerned, the end-in-view has to do with student learning; the desired result has to do with the "match" between what students have learned and what their teachers believe they have taught.

—Maxine Greene, 1984

BEYOND THE CLASSROOM

As Maxine Greene describes an "end-in-view," our thinking shifts from beyond the individual classroom to the scope of music teaching and learning over time. From a Comprehensive Musicianship through Performance (CMP) view, then, what is CMP *really*? Is it an approach? What do we mean by approach? Is it a model? Is it a philosophy? Is it a curricular framework? Is it a type of professional development? Is it a music education reform movement? How is it relevant to larger curricular issues, such as the national standards? While these questions have no single answer, they are important as we examine what CMP is and its connections beyond the classroom. This chapter will explore the larger issues related to CMP and the ways in which it can inform the music curriculum.

CMP is a framework for planning instruction that allows for the individual creativity and knowledge of the teacher to be realized. It is undergirded by principles about what it means to teach music and what it means to learn music—it is the learning piece that we don't always pay attention to. In other words, we often talk about technicalities of teaching music, organizing learning activities, selecting repertoire, and planning concerts. The CMP teacher goes about this work with the added awareness of the learning as experienced by students. This chapter zooms out for a broad consideration of CMP within a larger picture, one that includes students *and* teachers. We begin by looking at multiple facets of CMP: philosophy, approach, and process.

CMP as Philosophy

Curricula are informed by philosophical beliefs. Decisions about what to teach, how to teach it, and methods for assessing learning are all grounded in beliefs, whether at the level of a school district or individual teacher. A teacher-conductor who aspires toward a superior rating at a contest holds a certain set of beliefs and would make instructional decisions toward that end goal; a teacher-conductor who seeks to develop musical independence through student composition projects would have a different set of beliefs and make instructional decisions with a different end in sight. In what ways is CMP a philosophy? According to Bennett Reimer, "Every time a choice is made a belief is applied" (2003, p. 4). All that we do in the course of carrying out our teaching work reflects our beliefs about what we do. The myriad decisions are both large and small and are dependent upon our own understanding of music teaching and learning. Limited understanding or beliefs on the part of the teacher result in a hit-or-miss kind of musical experience for students rather than one that reflects deeper values. These choices ultimately impact students, and a leaning toward a CMP philosophy would agree with Boyle and Radocy that "all music students, regardless of age or musical locale, should have the opportunity to relate all aspects of their musical education to the total world of music" (1973, p. 2).

The original documents outlined in the original CMP proposal described several philosophical underpinnings, including a belief that musical independence as a performer, creator, and responder is an important outcome for students in performance classes; in-depth experiences in which students participate in a variety of musicianly roles, careful selection of repertoire, and a consistent effort to plan, organize, and implement the curriculum. The notion of rehearsal as laboratory in both performance and understanding is key in the implementation of a CMP philosophy—a setting in which teacher and students experience music in many varied ways, developing their own distinct musicianship (WMEA, 1977).

CMP as Approach

To think of *approach* or method is one of the ways we organize our thinking about particular ways to categorize instruction, including not only what should be taught, but *how*. In music education, when we think of approaches, some that come to mind include Orff-Schulwerk, Kodály, and Suzuki. Each has distinct features that provide for transmission of knowledge through a systematic plan as guided by a discrete philosophy. In addition to the methods listed there is a wide variety of texts used in music classrooms, many of which seek to align philosophy, goals, and activities. It is not uncommon for teachers to use many of these materials interchangeably in the ongoing search for the perfect fit for their students and situation.

In the case of CMP, it has a specific purpose, which emphasizes the interdependence of musical knowledge and musical performance. It is a program of instruction that seeks, through performance, to develop an understanding of basic musical concepts by involving students in a variety of roles and to enable students to synthesize material in all that they do (WMEA, 1977; Willoughby, 1971). CMP does not use a specific text or prescribe repertoire. A CMP teaching plan is centered on the music the teacher-conductor selects to explore, study, and perform. CMP, viewed as a pedagogical method like Orff-Schulwerk, forwards the idea that the approach is determined by the distinct music selected and the CMP plans developed and implemented by the teacher-conductor.

CMP as a Process

A third way to consider CMP in light of curricular matters is to view it as a process. Much discussion has ensued regarding the process and product aspects of teaching. Thinking about CMP as a process allows for the teacher to use her or his expertise to select repertoire and to create a teaching plan that forwards skill development, musical knowledge, and affective development, resulting in a highly personalized yet systematic approach in band, choir, and orchestra. A view of CMP as a process has more elasticity and allows and encourages the teacher to be creative in planning and teaching, to take risks, and to grow along with the students. *Process-ness* is also lived out in the classroom: teachers construct plans that demarcate each point of the model and details regarding each. However, as the plan is brought to life by teachers and students, those delineations give way to a musical experience that consists of performing with understanding (Sindberg, 2006). Emphasis on the experiences in the classroom and the process of learning music through performance are paramount.

THE CMP PRACTICE

The previous chapter described ways in which CMP can be enacted in the classroom through the implementation of a CMP teaching plan. Also included was a brief discussion of an approach to concert programming that builds upon a single work to include several works that provide focus for a unit of study or concert cycle. Both are mechanisms that contribute to a learning environment centered on comprehensive music learning and teaching. Let us consider, then, the classroom environment. Is there such a thing as a "CMP classroom"? What does that mean? What differences would one see between a CMP classroom and a non-CMP classroom? It's really about the feel of a classroom that values a comprehensive music experience—we recall the description of classroom as laboratory, a place where ideas are tried out and where the experiences are varied. Because "classroom" connotes a physical space, we will refer to the CMP practice, which also includes the teacher and students.

A CMP practice disrupts the traditional rehearsal structures and patterns in a number of ways. First, emphasis is placed on student learning through performance, rather than performance as the only goal. Many CMP practitioners refer to this as performing with understanding, which can result in a more satisfying and meaningful experience for students as well as the teacher-conductor. The CMP practice places a high value on student-centered activities. Two examples are listening squads and rehearsal critiques, both of which depend on students to evaluate the quality of their performance. In the case of a listening squad, a small group of students listens to the ensemble rehearse and offers constructive comments—this can be particularly effective with percussionists, who are occasionally less engaged than their counterparts on wind instruments. The ensemble rehearsal critique is completed by students as they evaluate, from their point of view, the performance of their ensemble, using a live performance or recorded performance. Because student ownership is so highly emphasized, the traditional[1] view of ensemble setting does not always fit comfortably within the CMP practice. The learning environment in a CMP practice is collaborative rather than corrective, inspired rather than instructive.

In addition, CMP, with its emphasis on student-centered strategies and shared learning, requires greater effort on the part of the teacher. Planning for student-centered learning places additional requirements on the teacher, particularly in terms of classroom management and selection of learning activities. It also decentralizes the power traditionally held by one person, and places it in the hands of the students (at least in part), which teachers may find threatening. Oftentimes ensemble directors are dealing with a larger number of students than in a regular classroom, and they may feel that the only way to maintain control is through autocratic methods; in reality if the teacher-conductor gives students ownership of the learning and there is collaboration between students, teachers, and the music, this results in deeper understanding and more quality performances. Ownership of learning, for example, can occur by having students actively participate in the musical analysis of a work individually or in small groups and shared with all students. Or through an invitation to students to share ideas about how to shape a particular musical phrase.

Teachers who have seen primarily the traditional model of instruction tend to replicate that model in their own ensembles. When teachers begin to experience the CMP planning process, the traditional model of music performance instruction is turned upside down.

While it is ultimately the responsibility of the teacher to make instructional decisions (she or he is the professional, trained in such matters, after all), the CMP practice encourages students to develop their own musical independence, through the planned process that is the CMP model.

CONSIDERING THE AFFECTIVE DIMENSION

Highlighting the affective dimension of the musical experience is an important component of the CMP practice. The difference with a CMP philosophy is that it is intentional and not left to chance or the assumption that it will just happen. This is challenging for teachers, because we may not have had models to help us see how to facilitate affective development in ensembles. We have had countless special moments that served to inspire when we were in school and collegiate ensembles, but when it comes to affective aspects of musical experience in the ensemble setting as teachers, this can be a difficult thing to give space to. The subjective nature of the affective, coupled with a fear of being vulnerable, may inhibit the sharing of personal feelings—on the part of the teacher as well as the students. It's like taking a trip—teacher-conductors, as the architects of the trip, know where we are going to go, and perhaps some of what we will see—and we want everyone to have a great time. We prepare students in advance with a deeper understanding of what they will experience, so that when they are in the moment, the affective experience will be richer, more significant.

One example of highlighting the affective comes from a high school choral rehearsal, in which students are studying "Musica Animam Tangens," by Shank (2005). The work is based on a poem by Newstrom and is included with his permission to help illuminate how it is used in relation to affect in a choral rehearsal.

> Music touching;
> Exhaling its breathless oceans of life
> Currents that free hearts giving love to
> All that open the sounds that fill
> The mountain of my existence
> And overflow my soul to touch
> God. (Shank, based on Newstrom, 2005)

Their teacher asks them to close their eyes. She reads the poem upon which the work is based and asks students to come up with a word to describe either the poem or the piece of music. She instructs students to have their word in mind as they sing through Shank's work, saying, "Make your word come to life when you sing." Next, students are invited to share their words—responses include "beautiful . . . peaceful . . . graceful . . . harmonious . . . eerie . . .

love." The teacher embraces each response with a nod and a smile. She asks students to sing again, keeping mindful of the various responses shared. The strategy of inviting students to form their own interpretation, shared with others, results in an environment where each person's viewpoint is valued. The teacher's outcome for this piece was for the students to explore their distinct interpretation of text and the ways in which music can amplify text. This example illustrates the ways a CMP teaching plan can facilitate an effective approach to the feelingful dimensions of the musical experience in the band, choir, and orchestra room.

CMP AND THE MUSIC CURRICULUM

Much of our discussion has been focused on CMP in relation to the individual teacher and her or his practice—writing and implementing a teaching plan, broadening the selection of repertoire in relation to concert programming, and working to center the musical experience on the students rather than from the podium. As we step back to take a wider view, we move into the space of the music curriculum as we consider ways in which CMP can inform and shape the music curriculum over the course of a year or multiple years, curricular applications across a school district, and link to national and state standards as well.

Long-Term Outcomes

There are many ways to view curriculum. Some may view curriculum as a series of classroom activities; for others it is a formalized course of study. The various ways of looking at curriculum, whether an ideal construct or a more pragmatic approach, suggest a set of planned experiences (Abeles, Hoffer, & Klotman, 1995). According to Lehman (1999), "The curriculum will be conceived not as a collection of activities in which students engage but rather as a well-planned sequence of learning experiences leading to clearly defined skills and knowledge" (p. 96). Continuity is commonly accepted as an important piece in the curriculum, taking place over time. Bruner argues that "the best way to create interest in a subject is to render it worth knowing . . . to make the knowledge gained usable in one's thinking beyond the situation in which the learning has occurred" (1977, p. 31). This knowledge needs to be connected and built on over time. Another source of curriculum development comes from the teacher's own professional growth.

A middle school band teacher, Peggy, was inspired after a semester's leave to create a type of outcome that she termed a "program outcome." When she returned to school, Peggy felt that her students were not playing as well as they should and that their level of motivation was inadequate. This inspired her to formulate a program outcome of *excellence* for the first quarter of the new school year, further demonstrating Peggy's level of initiative and yearning for quality by making pride and excellence a "big deal":

It was coming back and wanting a higher level, wanting things to be better. I feel like I want kids to desire excellence and have a pride about the program, that we are here [in band] because we want this to be good.

The wording of the outcome was included in Peggy's teaching plan: "Students will explore, define, and personalize a concept of excellence to use in their study of music in the first-quarter band curriculum" (Sindberg, 2006). She explained her rationale in an interview when asked to describe her plan and the ways this program outcome might be connected to CMP and the larger scope of the band curriculum. In this excerpt Peggy also framed that sense of excellence:

In order for someone to be excellent, they would have to understand what is ahead of them. They would have to have a knowledge of what it takes to be excellent, as opposed to me being the one who says, "That's not good enough, do better."

Peggy described her role as "creating an environment in which students take ownership for their own excellence." Her intent was to instill a higher level of performance as well as a disposition on the part of the students toward excellence. "The real thing I'm looking for in this excellence thing is their personal commitment to their betterment" (Sindberg, 2006). It was not only her standard of quality that she wanted students to assimilate; she also wanted her students to raise their own standards and expectations for their work over a period of time, establishing a disposition to excellence that would be long-lasting. This anecdote illustrates how a long-range goal can encourage investment on the part of both students and teacher. Pontious (2002) argues that it is just as important for the students to know where they are in relation to goals as it is for the teacher.

Standards and Standards-Based Curriculum

From June 1992 through June 1994, the Consortium of National Arts Education Associations developed voluntary national standards for music, visual arts, theater, and dance in grades K-12. These voluntary standards describe the knowledge, skills, and understanding that all students should acquire in the arts, providing a basis for developing curricula (Consortium of National Arts Education Associations, 1994). Introduced to music educators in 1994, the national standards were a seminal event in music education toward the end of the twentieth century. Part of the Goals 2000: Educate America Act, the standards solidified goals for K-12 music classrooms by identifying skills and knowledge necessary for musical literacy. This represents the first time the arts were recognized as a fundamental academic subject. Since the publication of the national standards, several states adopted their own version of standards—reform which subsequently found its way into local school districts and districtwide curricula. The CMP process organically aligns with national and state standards as part of the model, particularly assessment, outcomes, and strategies. Both CMP and the national standards are consonant in their advocacy for comprehensiveness.

Several additional resources are available to help generate ideas for teaching toward the standards. In *Performing with Understanding* Lehman argues that the national standards focus instructional goals and expectations, facilitate effective assessment, and align music with other subject areas as we claim a "share of the school curriculum" (Lehman, 2000, p. 9). He also reminds us that calling for every course in music to provide instruction in creating, performing, listening to, and analyzing music is an idea introduced by the Contemporary Music Project of Northwestern University (Lehman, 2000). Even though many ideas have been introduced in recent years in relation to curricular initiatives, the publication of the national standards has been instrumental in facilitating a more cohesive curriculum in grades K-12.

How do our national standards fit among the discussion of assessment, outcomes, and strategies as employed within CMP? Many state and district curricula have been developed based on the standards; while terminology may vary (e.g., outcomes, objectives, learning targets), the expectations of what students should learn and be able to do is increasingly tied to the national standards. Most curricula continue to view the standards as outcomes; however, a view through a CMP lens might look at the standards as strategies, and a teacher would apply those strategies to repertoire selected for the ensemble. Two examples help illustrate how we might view the nine standards applied as strategies.

Our first example utilizes composition. Students in a high school band are rehearsing "Ere the World Began to Be", by Jack Stamp (1996), which is based on a Gregorian chant. As they study the piece, students become familiar with chants as well as the way Stamp employs them. Students compose chants on their own, with the option of adding words. Over time and as the result of varied activities, they understand Gregorian chant and Stamp's use of chant in a contemporary idiom.

An example of using improvisation in a string orchestra is provided by Robert Gillespie in *Performing with Understanding* (2000). As students rehearse an arrangement of Bach's Brandenburg Concerto no. 3, invite them to improvise a melody using the D major chord as a basis, replicating Bach's use of only two chords in this short movement (Gillespie, 2000). By doing this, the ideas put forth in the national standards can be applied to *all* music studied in the ensemble setting. MENC has provided a number of resources specific to the band, choral, and orchestra settings that give examples of activities teachers can use, including *Teaching Examples: Ideas for Music Educators* (1994, now out of print). Many of the examples are available through the online lesson plan library My Music Class (www.nafme.org/lessons); search "strategies," and select the appropriate discipline. These resources are among the many that are available for teachers in search of new ideas.

Whether referred to as a standard, outcome, learning target, or strategy, the purpose of the examples provided is to engage students in composition and improvisation. The learning activities can be modified for other repertoire and for students in different contexts.

State and Local Curricula

One way that CMP can become infused in the music curriculum is to adopt it across a school building or district. This requires collaboration on the part of teachers working at the elementary, middle, and high school level. A comprehensive musicianship curriculum is an all-inclusive, multifaceted approach to developing musicianship: musical understanding, knowledge, and skills, individualizing instruction (Garofalo, 1983; Hylton, 1995) organized with continuity in mind. Several resources are available to assist in writing or revising curricula as a music department. *Music Curriculum Writing 101* (Odegaard, 2009) includes several suggestions for writing a standards-based curriculum. Additional resources include publications by state boards of education. An account of how one district worked to incorporate CMP into its curriculum is provided in the following anecdote.

Over the course of two years, one school district developed a plan to include CMP as a focus for the music curriculum. Music teachers participated in a day-long workshop with members of the CMP Committee, and teachers in the district attended the CMP summer workshop, all of which was supported by the district administration. During the school year, teachers wrote and implemented their teaching plans, talking about the learning that has taken place as a result of their experience. Selected teachers subsequently presented their work to the local school board and administrators, several of whom have commented positively about this districtwide initiative. Administrators began asking questions about the teaching plans and described a better understanding of what should be happening in the music program of this district. This example takes CMP well beyond the confines of the classroom walls and provides a useful model that can be replicated in other school districts.

CURRICULUM AND MUSIC SELECTION

As we take into account the music curriculum, whether specifically band, choir, or orchestra, we need to be mindful of balance. Within the context of the ensemble setting, this is particularly evident in music selection. Over the course of a year or multiple years, does the repertoire selected represent variety in terms of style, context, or historical period? What are the technical skills students need to develop? The teacher with an eye toward comprehensive musicianship will take this into account during the process of repertoire selection and be on the lookout for quality music that fulfills the potential for teaching comprehensively. The curriculum document prepared by a school district may be standards-based (increasingly the case); however, in the ensemble setting the teacher is responsible for selecting repertoire that aligns with district standards and expectations. Matters of repertoire selection and programming were addressed earlier; here we view those choices in relation to the longer view of the music curriculum. The selection of a masterwork, or centerpiece, in the program is described by Rachleff, who compares this to selecting literature as an English teacher might (Larsen, 2000). The goal is to use great art in balance with music that is technically challenging, stretches the audience, and inspires the hearts, brains, and fingers of our students (Larsen, 2000).

"The score is the nucleus from which all objectives flow" (Garofalo, 1983, p. 28) reminds us that the repertoire forms the basis of the curriculum in the ensemble. Like Labuta, Garofalo argues that a cyclical approach to repertoire selection would fuse long-term goals and repertoire selection, serve the needs of students, and fit within district-prescribed curricular expectations. In developing the national standards in 1994 a group of music educators considered what professional musicians do and developed a list of what students need to know and be able to do. These are long-range needs and should be the basis of the curriculum. Thus, the selection of music serves to help students achieve those curriculum outcomes and can also support a cyclical approach and use of a varied repertoire.

While student interest is an important element in learning, "if the music selected does not provide the students a well-defined focus on curricular goals (such as Standards), its use may be questionable as a valid learning medium" (Pontious, 2002). Repertoire selection must reflect a balanced diet that includes varied forms, styles, periods, and cultures—this was stated in the Tanglewood Declaration of 1967 and is included in the national standards as well. What does this look like as we consider curriculum and the ensemble? For example, there is a body of literature that, according to conventional wisdom, students need to experience while in the band program—a corpus of masterworks. The compositions of Holst, Vaughan Williams, and Grainger play an important role in the repertoire of the concert band—the centerpiece mentioned earlier. The notion that students should perform works by these composers to not only understand their role in the history of concert band, but to examine what it is about these works that establishes them as masterworks, has the potential for broad and deep learning about music. This is also the case in the orchestra and choral settings with their respective canon of masterworks. The main issue is breadth and depth, and this begins with repertoire selection. Arrangements and transcriptions can be used in ensembles with less-experienced students to form a bridge for learning about larger issues, as illustrated in earlier examples. Both have the potential for students to learn from high-quality music, providing it is age appropriate. These examples readily transfer among contexts.

National Standard #9, understanding music in relation to history and culture, provides an example of how a district curriculum could include a study of "masterwork" in contexts outside of music, such as visual art, literature, or pop culture. A study of "Ave Verum Corpus" could align with a study of Mozart and his role in music history, other composers of the Classical period, or visual art of the same era. The notion of what would be considered a "masterwork" in the realm of pop culture could demonstrate the transcendent qualities of a work that stands out and why. Related repertoire would be determined within the choir, band, or orchestra context, and in some cases that repertoire could cross over from one context to another.

Continuity has been cited as an important part of the implementation of curriculum and its impact on repertoire selection. Labuta supports a cyclical view that consists of a three- to four-year cycle focusing on the elements of music and diverse styles, historical periods, and cultures (1997). Garofalo (1983) advocates the "unit study composition" as a vehicle for incorporating musical knowledge, understanding, and skill. The unit study composition forms the centerpiece of the curriculum, facilitating a comprehensive musical experience. These examples help in our understanding of CMP applied over a period of several years, which helps to promote breadth and depth of musical experience. The quality of the musical experience and the ways in which it promotes the students' long-term mastery must always be part of our musical decisions and planning. This long-range focus is a natural result of the process of curriculum development (Abeles, Hoffer, & Klotman, 1995; Pontious, 2002).

CMP AND REFORM-MINDED MUSIC TEACHING

As this book goes to press, we find ourselves in another era of education reform, where legislative influences such as No Child Left Behind, financial crises, and social pressures impact life in schools. While music classrooms may not be the direct target of these efforts, they do impact the work of teachers and students. On the one hand, the notion of reform-mindedness in the music classroom could take the direction of satisfying expectations with regard to standardized testing and academic achievement. Increasingly, however, we see efforts that argue for a holistic approach to education, which includes music and the arts (Gardner, 2011; Pink, 2006; Ravitch, 2010), and these authors are among those who have shed important light on the essentialness of music and arts as components of a comprehensive education. In spite of the legislative, financial, and social milieu, those of us engaged in teaching music to children have an opportunity to promote and even celebrate the distinct ways music and arts contribute to the education of the whole child. In fact, now may be the ideal time to do just that.

The history of education and music education in the United States includes a vast array of initiatives, many of which served to act as a conduit for reform in music education. While many of these initiatives no longer exist in their original form, they have contributed to our continuing efforts to improve teaching and learning. Comprehensive musicianship is one example of an attempt to change music education, primarily through integrating various components of the music experience (Mark, 1996; Sindberg, 2006). CMP, as implemented, can be a way to transform the ways bands, orchestras, and choirs are taught and broaden to a large degree what students are learning in these performance-based classes—a setting in which traditions continue to hold fast.

One of the challenges facing teacher-conductors who seek to implement CMP in their band, choir, or orchestra room could be the nature of ensemble settings and traditions. We have addressed this in earlier chapters, but as we consider reform, it may be helpful to revisit those traditions and their impact on reform-minded music teaching. Typically, the decisions in an ensemble are made by the director; emphasis is placed on group performance rather than on the musical understanding of individual students (Burris, 1988; Dodson, 1989). Consequently, students form musical knowledge that is highly specific to responding to the conductor's wishes, and less so other forms of thinking. Reimer (2003) describes a "one-size-fits-all" level of understanding that may serve some students well, but others not at all (p. 220). These traditions create an additional challenge as one aims for a comprehensive musical experience for all students.

Curricular reform places additional demands upon teachers who are more stretched than ever before. Barrett (2005) talks about the paradox of teaching and how teachers are pulled in opposite directions, such as meeting the needs of an increasingly diverse student population while also standardizing instruction. As Barrett states, these challenges may be particularly well suited as we consider reshaping our view of curriculum. Reliance on grades and test scores is perhaps more important than ever before, and teachers are expected to employ multiple strategies for documenting student learning. Rather than viewing reform efforts as limitations imposed from outside, it is possible to see opportunities for imagining new alternatives.

The challenges we currently face, according to Barrett, cause a reexamination of habits and provide opportunities to think creatively about essential questions related to music teaching and learning in relation to what should be taught and how. Barrett invites us to think creatively about how these challenges might inspire a new vision of music curriculum. For example, she suggests placing the students' musical experience at the center of curriculum development, rather than the more prevalent sequential view of forming objectives, selecting learning experiences, delivering the curriculum, and evaluating student learning.

In addition to the national standards, reform efforts include emphasis on assessment and testing in an ongoing occurrence of change in education. With its framework and origins in classroom practice (see next chapter), CMP lends itself to new efforts without compromising solid educational practices, as in the case of Arts PROPEL (see chapter 2). In fact, CMP can help promote reform in the ensemble setting by encouraging a more student-centered culture.

In *Vision 2020*, a document addressing several contemporary issues related to music education in the twenty-first century, Lehman (1999) articulated the skills and knowledge required of teachers to enact a new curriculum informed by the national standards. Those skills and knowledge include knowing the students and the ways in which they develop, knowing their subject matter (particularly as it relates to the standards), and knowing how to organize and execute instruction effectively—including assessment.

As we consider reform within the context of the ensemble setting, we consider the ways in which CMP might forward change in the band, choir, and orchestra room. Several possibilities come to mind. First, with increased emphasis on musical understanding, students will develop better listening skills—their awareness will widen as they learn to focus their attention beyond their individual parts. A CMP-infused classroom will promote more creativity in thinking, interpreting, and creating music—students will more readily think in music. Ultimately, with an experience of the breadth and depth that CMP facilitates, we hope that students will be more likely to continue music making after leaving school. While none of these possibilities are particularly "new," the newness lies in their coming to life in the rehearsal room; in this way reform can take shape.

CONCLUSION

Maxine Greene uses the term "consciousness of craft" to describe a mindful view of our teaching work. Rather than being caught up in daily tasks and routines alone, she encourages us to also connect with and understand our students, their interests and concerns, and how our own mindfulness and reflections can serve as a model for our students. We may wonder why traditional rehearsal structures have remained largely the same since the beginning of school bands and orchestras—that is, the teacher on the podium, making most of the decisions: selecting repertoire, rehearsing, and evaluating the ensemble. In light of reform initiatives, why has so little seemed to change in the band, choir, and orchestra room? The model of music making at the university level is the highest possible level of performance. This model persists not only because of tradition; it is appropriate in that context. University students have many other music courses in which they learn about history, literature, and theory. In secondary schools, students have one class from which to learn music, making even stronger the case for a comprehensive music experience in the ensemble setting. There may be difficulty for music education graduates, as they enter the profession, to transpose that model into their particular teaching setting, which is highly unlikely to be at the same level of performance.

The cyclical nature of change is such that there is a recurrence of good ideas, and we have seen many examples. Many of the initiatives related to music curriculum are cyclical, but ultimately it can be reduced to *just good teaching*. While not a curriculum, CMP directly influences how a curriculum could be implemented and assessed in ways that forward students' musical understanding. By using standards as outcomes in the model/teaching plan, or as strategies to specific repertoire, the CMP model is essential to a planned, sequential study of music.

GOING FURTHER—QUESTIONS FOR DISCUSSION

1. What are some of the ways recent topics related to earlier music curricular initiatives?
2. Think of one to three strategies you could include to highlight the affective in a rehearsal.
3. What is the difference between the CMP model and a curriculum?
4. List four beliefs that you think CMP fosters.
5. In what ways would teacher education need to change to embrace principles of comprehensive musicianship through performance?

NOTE

1. The term *traditional* is used by several authors (Garofalo & Whaley, 1979; Sherburn, 1984; Swearingen, 1993), and is defined as a setting that emphasizes technically precise performance.

7

The Evolution of CMP

Our main hope was that we could move performing ensembles to a more comprehensive planning process that would broaden both the teaching and the learning in band, choir, and orchestra. The analogy to the technique-only typing class model is often used to describe what we wanted to move away from. (Schmid, 2007)

THE NEED FOR COMPREHENSIVE MUSICIANSHIP

Keene and Mark are among the authors who have written extensively in describing many of the developments and initiatives related to comprehensive musicianship (Keene, 1987; Mark, 1996). This chapter describes the evolution of the Comprehensive Musicianship through Performance (CMP) Project, the outgrowth of a collective vision of a group of music educators and its connection to earlier initiatives. The need for comprehensive musicianship was articulated by Abeles, Hoffer, and Klotman:

Stated more in relation to the specifics of ensemble settings, performance is not a sufficient end to justify maintaining school music programs. It should be a means toward obtaining musical literacy and musical understanding. It was with this goal in mind that comprehensive musicianship became a significant force for the teaching of music in the 1960s and 1970s. (1984, p. 282)

The purpose of this chapter is to trace the unique outcomes that resulted from the collective vision of the founders of the Wisconsin Comprehensive Musicianship through Performance (CMP) Project; an example of holistic music teaching and learning in the ensemble setting that emerged from best practices and principles of comprehensive musicianship during a climate of education reform in the post-Sputnik era.[1] The voices of some of the participants in the initial planning meetings are included to help illuminate the distinct process that led to the first CMP model.[2]

In 1977, a group of music educators met at a small liberal arts college in the upper Midwest. These music educators gathered together to examine music teaching and learning in performing ensembles. While they were well aware that students in their particular region played and sang with technical prowess, these music educators believed in the possibility of broadening the musical experience for students in band, choir, and orchestra. Perhaps, they imagined, something like general music in the elementary school—where students often sang, played instruments, and listened to music. They envisioned a musical experience with breadth and depth that was multifaceted and would more fully engage students in the ensemble setting. Their ideas were not isolated; rather, they were inspired by earlier events both in music education and in general education. These music educators sought to transpose selected elements of these events to the ensemble setting during a period of educational reform in the mid-20th century, a time in which a perception of Soviet superiority led to increased emphasis on improving the educational system in the United States.

SIGNIFICANT EVENTS THAT INFORMED THE CMP PROJECT

Of the many initiatives in *contemporary*[3] music education of the post-Sputnik era, four were particularly significant leading up to the 1977 meeting. These initiatives were the Contemporary Music Project, the Manhattanville Music Curriculum Program, Yale Seminar, and Tanglewood Symposium.

Contemporary Music Project

In 1959, inspired by an idea forwarded by Norman Dello Joio, the Young Composers Project began. Sponsored by the Ford Foundation, this project placed composers in the public schools for the purpose of composing for the schools' performance ensembles. The Young Composers Project was so successful that the Ford Foundation expanded and elevated it to one of its ten major projects, which carried a substantial increase in funding (Mark, 1996). This project was the direct predecessor to the Contemporary Music Project, begun in 1963. The expanded program was named the Contemporary Music Project for Creativity in Music Education (shortened to Contemporary Music Project), and the Young Composers Project became known as Composers in Public Schools. Among the goals MENC created for the program were:

1. To increase the emphasis on the creative aspect of music in the public schools;
2. To create a solid foundation or environment in the music education profession for the acceptance, through understanding, of the contemporary music idiom;
3. To reduce the compartmentalization that now exists between the profession of music composition and music education for the benefit of composers and music educators alike;
4. To cultivate taste and discrimination on the part of music educators and students regarding the quality of contemporary music used in schools; and
5. To discover, when possible, creative talent among students (*CMP in Perspective*, 1973, p. 34).

The Contemporary Music Project took place between 1963 and 1969 and was cosponsored by MENC and the Ford Foundation. It sought to expand and broaden the efforts initiated by the Young Composers Project. One of the significant contributions of this project was a body of repertoire created for school performing groups. A second contribution was the opportunity for students to participate in the creative process, through working with composers in their schools. It was the original Contemporary Music Project that led to the Seminar on Comprehensive Musicianship at Northwestern University in 1965, a meeting organized to improve the musical education of teachers by looking at required college core courses in music theory and history. The most significant result of this seminar was the introduction of the term *comprehensive musicianship*. The Northwestern Seminar is recognized as having established a set of principles for the reform of the undergraduate music curricula, according to Mark (1996) and Willoughby (1971).

Manhattanville Music Curriculum Project

The Manhattanville Music Curriculum Program (MMCP) was of particular significance to the leaders of the 1977 meeting mentioned in the introduction. The MMCP began in 1965, under the direction of Ronald Thomas. The primary goal of this project was to broaden the musical experience for students in grades K-12 chiefly through development of a sequential curriculum (Thomas, 1970). This program consisted of three phases. Phase One examined traditional music education practices, including curriculum and the ways students learned. The second phase included the development of a spiral curriculum, modeled after Bruner (1977). The curriculum consisted of a sequence of musical concepts presented multiple times at various stages of development. The third phase of the MMCP consisted of teacher inservice programs presented in the form of curriculum guides and professional development workshops for teachers. The project, funded by the U.S. Department of Education, lasted six years.

The Yale Seminar and Tanglewood Symposium

The Yale Seminar took place in 1963 and sought to examine the challenges facing music education, particularly in light of an emphasis on science curriculum. Participants at the Yale Seminar included musicians, scholars, and teachers who sought to both broaden the repertoire for study in schools and deepen the experience through more comprehensive study. Held in 1967, the Tanglewood Symposium was a seminal event that challenged almost all of the basic tenets on which music education in the schools was based. One of the most important outcomes of the symposium was the Tanglewood Declaration, a document that called for music to be placed at the center of the school curriculum. Although the Tanglewood Symposium did not address comprehensive musicianship directly, it was a strong force for broadening the types of music studied, paying more attention to the musical needs of individual students, and changing the nature of music teacher preparation (Mark, 2000).

The Yale Seminar and Tanglewood Symposium were two important pivotal events in the contemporary era of music education (Mark, 1996). The Manhattanville Music Curriculum Program, with its emphasis on professional development and spiral curriculum, provided a picture of classroom implementation of comprehensive musicianship. In addition to the Contemporary Music Project, these initiatives laid the foundation for the comprehensive musicianship movement. Thus, the idea of introducing contemporary Western art music to public school students had evolved to a more in-depth view of music teaching and learning, more specifically, defining and redefining the principles and practices involved in the teaching of comprehensive musicianship. Among these are the emphasis on understanding the elements of music; the interdisciplinary study of theory, history, and performance; the involvement of students in musicianly roles such as performer, composer, conductor, listener, and analyst; and the practice of ensemble classes that function as both learning laboratories and rehearsal settings (Garofalo, 1983; Heisinger, 1991; Labuta, 1997; Wisconsin Music Educators Association, 1977; Woods, 1972).

A VISION TAKES SHAPE

In 1972, Charles Benner wrote *Teaching Performing Groups* (Benner, 1972). This document contained an extensive review of literature related to the various aspects of teaching performing groups. According to Benner, performing groups are the dominant musical structure in most secondary schools and the place where the most music teaching and learning takes place; those groups emphasize skill development. In addition to the development of performance skills, Benner suggested that a planned effort on the part of the teacher can enrich the performing experience with additional kinds of understanding, such as knowledge of history and literature (Benner, 1972). Those involved in the 1977 meeting embraced Benner's conclusions about the limited impact on music learning of participation in school performing groups.

The events begun in 1977 were influenced by the energy, inspiration, and momentum of new educational initiatives described earlier. Leaders of three organizations formed the original steering committee of what was to become the CMP Project and subsequent model: Mike George of the Wisconsin Department of Public Instruction, Richard Gaarder of the Wisconsin School Music Association, and Will Schmid of the Wisconsin Music Educators Conference. Their discussions during the planning stages focused on new possibilities in the face of traditional practices. Schmid described the initial hopes of the steering committee in the quotation at the opening of this chapter, restated here: "Our main hope was that we could move performing ensembles to a more comprehensive planning process that would broaden both the teaching and the learning in band, choir, and orchestra. The analogy to the technique-only typing class model is often used to describe what we wanted to move away from." From the very beginning, there was a vision for something different in the rehearsal room than had been the tradition.

Three goals were central at the early planning stages: collaboration of three state organizations related to education, broadening teaching and learning in the ensemble setting, and selecting music teachers perceived as achieving excellence in the eyes of their peers. The shared effort by these organizations sought to initiate change in philosophy, goals, and strategies for music education through performing groups; such collaboration was unusual. It also set this effort apart from other forms of comprehensive musicianship (M. George, personal communication, 2007; W. Schmid, personal communication, 2007). The collaboration of the Wisconsin Department of Public Instruction, Wisconsin Music Educators Association, and the Wisconsin School Music Association[4] expanded the reach and credibility of the project immediately, according to George.

A project steering committee made up of representatives from the three organizations discussed the form that this project might take in its initial stages. They began to codify the format of the project, beginning with the selection of teacher-participants. In 1976 a letter and nomination form were sent to all middle and high school band and choir directors in Wisconsin, who were invited to nominate one or more directors to be a part of the project. Several criteria were provided, the most important being the performance level of the teacher-participant's band or choir.[5] Among those factors most critical in the formative stages of the project was selection of music teachers who were achieving excellence in the eyes of their peers. "Working out a process for planning instruction with solid teacher-practitioners grounded us and laid the foundation for wide acceptance by their teaching peers" (Schmid, 2007). George, Gaarder, and Schmid envisioned reform at a grassroots level, emerging from the classroom and reaching outward.

THE FIRST SUMMER INSTITUTE AND
DEVELOPMENT OF A TWO-YEAR PILOT PROJECT

"When the first CMP committee met in 1977, we said from the outset that we wanted to look at process, find common elements that excellent music teachers used, and avoid dictating literature or outcomes" (M. George, personal communication, 2007). Goals of the first summer meeting included building a team of teacher advocates, developing a model and strategies, learning from each other, and constructing a long-range plan for moving forward. George described the organic process of the 1977 institute:

> We had no model at the time but we had a carefully planned institute that required teachers to do a lot of self-analysis (not evaluation) of their own teaching and how they accomplished their goals. Participants were encouraged to challenge one another, and there were some tense moments—including the possibility of a "mutiny" by a couple of choral directors. However, Will and I listened carefully, and looked for patterns or themes in the instructional planning process. By the third day, we had the first draft of the *CMP Model for Planning Instruction*. It grew from the insights and analysis by the participants (George, 2007).

Eight teachers were selected by the steering committee to participate in the institute and for an initial, two-year pilot project: two middle school band, two middle school choral, two high school band, and two high school choral. During this period, the eight teachers and members of the steering committee examined teaching practices in order to "identify common elements that excellent music teachers used" (George, 2007). One of the teacher-participants was Peter Schmalz, who described the primary topic of discussion as the combining of performance with an in-depth study of music; there were no definite ideas set. "The initial meeting brought people together to talk about how they, as a group, might work toward comprehensive musicianship. The chief goal was to move beyond performance" (P. Schmalz, personal communication, 2008). The group discussed the importance of repertoire selection and developed a planning model for instruction in performing groups. Next, they analyzed selected scores and created outcomes and strategies. This process resulted in teaching plans that were subsequently implemented by the teacher-participants in their respective programs. Discussions took place in small groups and large groups, allowing for all participants to contribute (P. Schmalz, personal communication, 2008).

Jan Tweed, who taught junior high band, was another teacher who participated in the first meeting. She described her experience at the 1977 meeting as among "the most stressful, exciting, and thought-provoking" of her teaching career (J. Tweed, personal communication, 2007). Tweed echoed George's and Schmalz's descriptions of the discussions at the institute, indicating they were peppered with lively exchanges among teachers with strong opinions, teaching philosophies, and passion. "I grew up with the philosophy that the teacher was the person to impart knowledge and students were the recipients" (J. Tweed, personal communication, 2007). To realize that CMP would forge a shift toward more active involvement for students inspired Tweed to renew her passion for teaching. The experience of coming to consensus with this new group of colleagues in an effort to make learning more meaningful remained with her for the rest of her teaching career. Her renewed enthusiasm and resolve to implement the CMP model helped her grow as a teacher, both in her classroom and as a member of the CMP Project, instructing teachers at the CMP workshops, inservices, and national presentations.

CMP was introduced in a document that outlined the rationale and founding principles of this project. It was co-authored by Michael George, Richard Gaarder, and Will Schmid:

> Comprehensive musicianship is defined as a program of instruction which emphasizes the interdependence of musical knowledge and musical performance. It is a program of instruction that seeks, through performance, to develop an understanding of basic musical concepts: tone, melody, rhythm, harmony, texture, expression, and form. This is done by involving students in a variety of roles including performing, improvising, composing, transcribing, arranging, conducting, rehearsing, and visually and aurally analyzing music. (Wisconsin Music Educators Association, 1977)

OUTCOME OF THE 1977 INSTITUTE: THE CMP MODEL

Following three days of intense discussion, debate, and a bit of drama, the first draft of the *CMP Model for Planning Instruction* was created. According to George, "It grew from the insights and analysis of the participants" (George, 2007). The group also articulated a set of beliefs:

- Musical independence as a performer, creator, and responder is an important outcome for students in performance classes;
- Careful planning for instruction leads to more comprehensive, meaningful student learning;

- Rehearsals utilizing a variety of educational strategies and environments can increase in-depth learning about music;
- The quality of music selected affects the breadth and lasting impact of learning;
- Assessment of learning by teachers and students is essential at all stages of the experience (before, during, and after);
- Comprehensive teaching, where students take initiative for their own learning, often produces creative results that exceed expectations. (Wisconsin Music Educators Association, undated)

Figure 7.1 depicts the original diagram of the CMP model. With the exception of *objectives*, currently included as outcomes, the planning points have remained consistent. What is interesting in this diagram is the intersecting lines throughout, showing an interconnectedness and flexibility unlike other teaching models. This is not a sequential diagram, nor is it ordered. One can begin at any point and move to another as best suits the needs of the teacher and students.

COMPREHENSIVE *M*USICIANSHIP THROUGH *P*ERFORMANCE

A Statewide Project of the
WISCONSIN DEPARTMENT OF PUBLIC INSTRUCTION
WISCONSIN SCHOOL MUSIC ASSOCIATION
WISCONSIN MUSIC EDUCATORS CONFERENCE

A MODEL FOR PLANNING INSTRUCTION

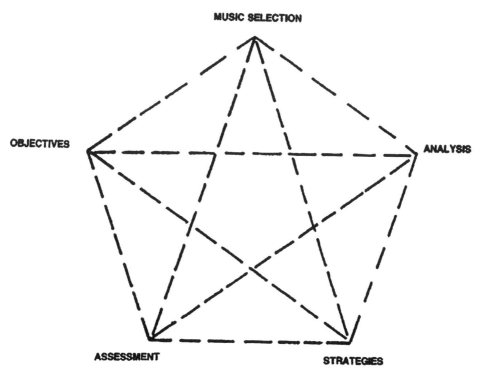

Figure 7.1. Original CMP Model Diagram

During the two-year pilot program, several meetings took place to discuss the implementation of the teaching plans and related matters. Teachers on the original project kept logs describing the ways they put these ideas into practice, applying the model to one or two pieces initially. They kept records of ideas tried and the effects those ideas had on students. Members of the steering committee also conducted on-site visits. The on-site visits revealed three common insights about students' learning in classrooms where the model was used:

- Students learned more than teachers expected or realized;
- Student attitudes toward CMP involvement varied, but were generally positive;
- The variety and scope of performing groups' experiences and strategies increased considerably [in comparison to those who were not grounded in the CMP experience]. (Wisconsin Music Educators Association, undated)

The CMP Project and model emerged from the belief that performing groups, not general music, constitute the foundation of the school music program in most middle and high schools. Consequently, performing groups were the primary settings from which to develop and implement comprehensive musicianship—in the case of the Wisconsin Project, performing with understanding.

Schmalz indicated that his involvement with CMP resulted in an increased scrutiny and selectivity in relation to music selection. "The CMP Model emphasized selecting literature that was rich in teaching possibilities and musical heft" (P. Schmalz, personal communication, 2008). Unlike other forms of comprehensive musicianship, the framework of the CMP model takes teachers through a planning process using repertoire that they select, and is further personalized through the remaining points of the model. The CMP model has undergone only slight modifications in appearance since 1977; the content has remained consistent.

The beliefs articulated by the participants at the 1977 meeting have a familiar ring to those acquainted with other forms of comprehensive musicianship, including the interdisciplinary study of music as well as student involvement in varied musicianly roles (Choksy, Abramson, Gillespie, Woods, & York, 2001; Sindberg, 2006). The most significant difference from the standpoint of the CMP model is the emphasis on the ensemble setting.

CONCLUSION

Comprehensive musicianship is a movement that has existed over several decades in several guises with some unifying attributes and some distinct qualities, depending on the form that it takes. The term itself, *comprehensive musicianship*, continues to be widely used among music educators, a use that would be worth examining in detail: What does the term *comprehensive musicianship* mean? As in the opening paragraphs of this book where we asked what and where good teaching is, the question is not so easy to answer; the value lies in the asking.

At the heart of comprehensive musicianship is a desire to expand what teachers teach, what students learn, and the way they participate in their learning. CMP is not the only initiative that descended from the Contemporary Music Project and its contemporaries, nor is it the only effort that promoted a broad and deep musical experience for students in the classroom. The Hawaii Music Curriculum Program (Thomson, 1970), *Blueprint for Band* (Garofalo, 1983), and *Teaching Musicianship in the High School Band* (Labuta, 1997) included curricular materials designed to foster musical understanding. Those materials are additional contributions intended to deepen student learning in the ensemble. Other initiatives informed the 1977 institute and subsequent formation of the CMP Project and model in addition to the Contemporary Music Project, Yale Seminar, Tanglewood Symposium, and Manhattanville Music Curriculum Program.

Its organic beginning, from shared conversations among Dick Gaarder, Mike George, and Will Schmid and the eight teachers brought together in 1977 to examine what excellent music teachers were doing in their rehearsals, is one of the significant differences that sets CMP apart from other comprehensive musicianship initiatives. Other differences have been described in earlier chapters, as well as the anecdotes of teacher-conductors versed in CMP. The acronym CMP today stands for Comprehensive Musicianship through Performance and not Contemporary Music Project. This long-lasting emphasis on changing how musical performance classes are taught has outlasted most previous initiatives across the country. Could this be because it originated from and is designed to evolve from music teachers who are actually doing the teaching?

Did the original CMP steering committee envision what would happen as a result of their conversations thirty years ago? "I really don't believe anyone, including the steering committee, had any idea of the scope and depth and impact of this project over the years" (J. Tweed, personal communication, 2007). This continuation of using music teachers in the field has helped the project grow and maintain its integrity while also contributing to its longevity.

While the full impact of CMP on teachers and students in the ensemble setting is not fully known, teachers continue to participate in professional development efforts such as conferences and workshops. In addition, teacher-educators share examples of the ways they include comprehensive musicianship in their methods courses and through publications. These examples are evidence of ongoing attempts to bring more into the musical experience for students. They are efforts that point to a desire to facilitate a richer experience and a change in the ensemble setting from performance to performance with *understanding*. Mike George, one of the founding fathers of the Wisconsin CMP Project participated in a recent online conversation among CMP Project members, the topic of which was helping teachers move beyond the "*how* to do CMP" issues to more substantive matters of "*why* to use CMP."

> "Why CMP" is too big a question. Change comes in increments. A teacher will gain greater understanding through the CMP process and model if each time a teaching strategy or behavior is shared it is accompanied with an explanation of *why*—going beyond what you do to *why* you do what you do. And asking that same question of teachers when they present their plans will expand their understanding of the teaching/learning process as it relates to CMP.

Change can come slowly to the ensemble setting, but it is possible. The kinds of changes that CMP promotes do not lessen the quality of experience; rather, they can bring about a deeper musical experience for students and richer, more meaningful challenges for teachers.

NOTES

1. A perception of Soviet superiority led to increased emphasis on improving the educational system in the United States, and with that emphasis came increases in funding for math, science, reading, and eventually, music and the arts. Passage of the National Defense Education Act led to increased funding for math, science, and other curricular areas, including music education.

2. Much of the content of this chapter is excerpted from an article printed in *Contributions to Music Education*, a publication of the Ohio Music Education Association, Birch Browning, editor (Sindberg, 2009). Printed with permission.

3. While no longer contemporary in relation to currency, I use the term to describe this era, which Mark (1996) referred to as "contemporary music education" (p. 28).

4. The Wisconsin Department of Public Instruction is a governmental agency sponsored by the State of Wisconsin; Wisconsin Music Educators Association (formerly known as the Wisconsin Music Educators Conference) is a professional organization of music teachers; the Wisconsin School Music Association exists to serve schools and students in Wisconsin.

5. The pilot project consisted of band and choir teachers. Orchestra teachers were added after the pilot phase.

Appendix A

Battalia for Strings (Score Excerpts),
Heinrich Ignaz Franz Biber, ed. Joel Blahnik

Battalia

Heinz Ignaz Franz Biber
edited by Joel Blahnik

The Dissolute Gathering of Musketeers, the March, the Battle, the
Lament of the Wounded, matched with Arias and dedicated to Bacchus

1. Sonata

* Strike the side of the instrument with the wood of the bow.

Figure A.1. Movement 1[1]

2. The Profligate Society of Common Humour

3.

4. The March

* The bass imitates a drum by weaving a piece of paper under the A string and over the E and D strings.

Figure A.2. Movements 2, 3, 4

* Not to be struck with the bow, but rather with the right hand snapping the string (Bartók pizzicato) against the fingerboard, and loud! (to imitate cannons)

Figure A.3. Movements 5, 6, 7

8. The Lament of the Wounded

Figure A.4.   Movement 8

NOTE

1. These excerpts are provided to help illuminate aspects of this work as described in chapter 1. The entire first movement and the first several measures of each subsequent movement are included.

Appendix B

CMP Teaching Plan Worksheets

These workshop planning sheets are used in the construction of a CMP teaching plan.

Music Selection

Does the composition teach?
What does it teach?
What do your students need?
Will the knowledge they gain from the composition be transferable?
Does the composition challenge your students technically?
Does the piece have aesthetic value?
Criteria for the selection of music
Composer/arranger/publisher

Programming

Length   Audience   Special events   Community

Aesthetic Effect/Musical Effect/Affective Response
Level of Difficulty

Maturity   Technique   Rehearsal demands

Personnel

Voicing   Range   Instrumentation   Solos

Musical Elements

Rhythm   Melody   Harmony   Form
Timbre   Texture   Expression

Personal Satisfaction

Teacher
Students

Additional Criteria
Historic and cultural connections
Related arts
Needs of the total curriculum
Additional choral criteria
Text: poem, foreign language, word meaning, tone painting
Accompaniment: characteristics, difficulty, relationship of voices/instruments

Analysis

How would you describe this composition?

Don't answer this question too quickly, for the answer may affect the rest of your analysis.

What type of composition is this?

(Suite, motet, overture, etc.)

What compositional devices are used?

(Repetition, contrast, augmentation, dimunition, motivic development, canon, etc.)

How are musical elements utilized?

Expression	Melody
Form	Texture
Harmony	Timbre
Rhythm	

What combination of musical ideas leads to this being a quality composition?

What makes it worth rehearsing and performing?

Consider the value of the music in relationship to the rehearsal time available.

What musical/cultural traditions does the piece represent?

What historical connections can you draw from the composition?

How good is the edition? Is it historically accurate?

How does the text contribute to the overall effect of the composition?

What is the heart of the piece?

The heart of a piece is the motor that gives it life—the most important element. If the piece has no heart (like the tin man), it probably isn't worth performing.

Outcomes

What do you want students to learn?

Feelings
Knowledge
Skills
(When writing outcomes, it helps to think about observable behaviors.)

Musicianly roles for use in writing outcomes

Assess	Identify	Read
Analyze	Improvise	Reflect
Arrange	Listen	Research
Compose	Move	Respond
Conduct	Notate	Sing
Discuss	Play	Write
Evaluate		

Keep in mind important long-range goals
   Musical independence
   Experience with a balanced selection of literature
   Lifelong involvement with music
Outcomes may involve the use of several compositions.
Possible sources for outcomes
   Music selection
   State and national standards
   Curriculum
   Musical elements
   Editor/composer notes

Sample outcome: *Students will identify and describe sonata-allegro form.*

Strategies

How can you facilitate student learning?
What learning activities will you use?
  Connect strategies to outcomes
Consider these basic ways to learn

Abstract	Student-centered
Aural	Tactile
Interdisciplinary	Verbal
Kinesthetic	Visual

Consider these activities for presenting strategies

Analyzing	Evaluating	Playing
Arranging	Identifying	Reading
Bowing	Improvising	Reflecting
Clapping	Journaling	Researching
Classifying	Listening	Scoring
Composing	Moving	Sight reading
Describing	Notating	Singing
Discussing	Orchestrating	Verbalizing

Strategies outside of school

Music in other classes	Reading
Researching	Interviewing
Field trips	Listening

Use metaphors, analogies, and similes to make your point
  (Examples include food, nature, sports)
During concerts, emphasize the learning that has led up to the event
Consider strategies for creative concert performances

Assessment

Before
  What are your students' goals?
  What do your students feel they need to work on?
  What do you think the students need to work on?
During
  What are your students' perceptions of their progress so far?
  In the learning process how close are you to your agreed-upon goals?
  How do your students feel about what they are doing?
  Have you encountered any new learning opportunities?
After
  Develop student portfolios showing student growth as comprehensive musicians
  Critique your own performance (concert performance or individual work)
  Critique others' performances
  Discuss the value of the experience
  Paper and pencil exams
  Observe attitude, skill and knowledge development
  Check assignments
Have students perform in small ensembles and critique each other.
How well do they generalize those learnings to other pieces of music?
Are students becoming mature, independent musicians?
Do your students continue to sing, play, and use music throughout the rest of their lives?

Appendix C

CMP Teaching Plan, *Battalia*

Gary Wolfman[1]

BATTALIA BY HEINRICH IGNAZ FRANZ BIBER, ED. JOEL BLAHNIK

CMP Teaching Plan

Heinrich Biber (1644–1704) was born in Prague and later spent twenty-four years in Salzburg serving as Kapellmeister for the court of the archbishop of Salzburg. Biber was described by noted violin maker Jacob Stainer as "the outstanding virtuoso Herr Biber." Well known as a great violinist, he became best known as a composer of violin works, many of which employ scordatura (unconventional tunings of the violin strings). His "Rosary Sonatas" consisted of sixteen sonatas, each of which had a different tuning of the open strings. Biber's music used canonic devices and diverse harmonic techniques, polytonality, and *col legno* that predate the later Baroque works of Pachelbel and J. S. Bach.

Battalia, edited by Wisconsin native Joel Blahnik, was originally written in 1673 during the Baroque era. Some historians attributed this work as Biber's sentiments toward the Thirty Years' War. This was a religious war fought from 1618 to 1648 that involved most of Europe. It began as a conflict between Protestants and Catholics and spread throughout many European countries. The war often used mercenary armies and created much famine and disease that devastated many countries. Biber might have expressed serious feelings about the war, as it was recorded that nearly half of the male population of German states and over a third of Czechs were killed. Biber grew up in the Czech area and spent his adulthood in the German state of Austria. *Battalia* is a statement reflecting various aspects of war, such as the social and historical impact of war and its toll on humanity.

Analysis

Battalia is often translated as "a body of troops" or simply as "battle." The work is dedicated to Bacchus, god of wine, vegetation, and theater. This immediately suggests notions of absurdity to both player and listener. Biber uses many nontraditional techniques, including striking the bow on the instrument, paper woven through strings, and Ives-like polytonality. The piece is divided into eight short movements with the following titles:

1. "Sonata"
2. "The Profligate Society of Common Humor"
3. "Allegro"
4. "The March"
5. "Presto"
6. "Aria"
7. "The Battle"
8. "The Lament of the Wounded"

1. "Sonata" (Gathering of the troops[2])
   AB form. The A section uses a rhythmic motive, which suggests the marching of troops to a central gathering place. Biber uses other motives to represent different groups. For example, what is the example that is to be included here? The B section uses dynamics to create a call and response pattern, perhaps representative of different groups engaging in dialogue. A new timbre is introduced by using the wood of the bow against the side of the instrument.
2. "The Profligate Society of Common Humor" (The troops have gathered in one location, each at its own campsite)
   The form of this movement includes eight different songs, each starting at a different time. Polytonality is the primary harmonic device, with the eight melodies presented in seven different keys (D, c, d, F, A, G, e). Rhythmic intensity results from Biber's use of 12/8 and 4/4 simultaneously. One imagines each mercenary group singing its own theme at the same time at this campsite.
3. "Allegro" (An interlude as troops pass the time before the battle)
   The form is AA BB; dynamic scheme is *f-p-f-p*. The movement is in D major. Its brevity—only seven measures long—may express feelings of uneasiness as the troops wait for battle. They may be feeling fearful and anxious, but outside they show a sense of frivolity and bravado.
4. "The March" (A military leader stepping forward to organize and lead the troops)
   This movement consists of a violin solo with a single bass accompaniment. The key is D major, but the violin part includes a G-sharp intentional, making it in A. The bass player imitates a drum by weaving a piece of paper under the A string and over the D and E strings.
5. "Presto" (Happiness and bravura before battle)
   Form of this movement is A B Development [using canon] B B. It is in D major and some A major. Dynamic scheme is *f-p-f-p-f*. This movement is in triple meter, dotted-half=76.
6. "Aria" (Prayer before battle)
   Form is A A B B. Begins in D major, moves to A major, and concludes in D major. This movement is very reflective in style and tempo. All parts have moving and weaving lines as if each individual soldier has his own thoughts.
7. "The Battle" (No explanation needed)
   Form is A B A B. Rhythmic motive uses repeated sixteenth notes.
8. "The Lament of the Wounded" (A part of the war that is often forgotten)
   Uses a rhythmic motive that suggests dragging of a wounded leg. The movement begins in B minor and ends in D major, possibly to symbolize hope after the war is over. Great harmonic dissonance in m. 11 and 12, using chromatics and suspensions. Dynamic range is *p-pp*.

The Heart

The heart of *Battalia* is the way the composer expresses the different aspects of war by using traditional and nontraditional musical effects, creating a multitude of emotional timbres.

Outcomes

1. Students will demonstrate the bowing style of the Baroque period and be able to create exceptions to the basic rules (skill).
2. Students will be able to describe and identify the musical concepts of polytonality and polymeter (knowledge).
3. Students will be able to express and describe how music can capture the many emotions of war (affective).

Strategies for Outcome 1

1. Play a recording of music from the Baroque period and have students identify and write in their portfolios the bowing styles they hear.
2. Go around the room and have each student create a unique sound using their instrument.
3. Have students locate the unique sounds in *Battalia* and then try them out.

Strategies for Outcome 2

1. Have the students play "Twinkle, Twinkle, Little Star" with each string section starting on a different pitch. Then have each section create and play a variation of "Twinkle" with at least one group using triplets.

2. After the students have learned the notes and rhythms to the second movement of *Battalia*, have each part (there are eight) spread out throughout the entire rehearsal space (each part should be as far apart as possible from the other parts). Then play the second movement from this position. Ask the students, "Why did the composer write eight parts in seven keys?"

3. Using an established set of bowing exercises in warm-ups, have each section play the exercises in different keys. Then separate the sections from each other by one or two beats.

4. Have each section come up with its own theme song. After each group has played their song for the orchestra, have them all play them together.

Strategies for Outcome 3

1. Lead a discussion on the following question: "Is Biber in favor of war or against war, and why? Why do you think Biber dedicated this piece to Bacchus?"

2. After playing the movement "Aria" from *Battalia*, have the students write a letter home as if they would be in battle the very next day.

3. After the students know *Battalia* well, have them work in small groups to try to figure out what Biber might have been saying about war in each movement. Then have a class discussion in which students share their ideas.

Assessment for Outcome 1

1. Hand out another piece from the Baroque period and see if the students can sight read the piece using traditional Baroque bowings.

2. Have the students compare and contrast a different Baroque piece from the Biber.

Assessment for Outcome 2

1. Give the students a simple melody written on paper or on the board and have them rewrite it in two different keys of their choice. Then play the melody together in the keys they have written.

2. Divide the students into groups of eight and have them compose a rhythmic piece by layering the music, like African drumming. Have one student in each group keep a steady beat and each student create a rhythmic motive that fits within that beat. Keep adding one student at a time in each group. Then perform them for the class.

Assessment for Outcome 3

1. On a written exam, have the students describe how Biber musically captured the emotions of war in *Battalia*.

2. Have the students write in their portfolios their thoughts on the following question: "If Biber was alive today, how might his music about war sound different or the same?" Discuss responses in class.

Music Selection

1. Since our country is at war presently, this piece might help the students explore the different emotions they might have about war.

2. *Battalia* is a good piece to explore ways in which composers followed the basic music rules of their time and how they introduced new and sometimes controversial ideas.

3. This composition has excellent examples of polytonality and polyrhythm.

NOTES

1. Gary Wolfman was the orchestra director at North and West High Schools in Appleton, Wisconsin, where he successfully implemented Comprehensive Musicianship through Performance while maintaining performance excellence in his ensembles. He is a former chair of the CMP Project and has served on the project since 1980.

2. Parenthetical references represent interpretive comments by Gary Wolfman.

Appendix D

CMP Teaching Plan, "Orpheus with His Lute"

Miriam Altman[1]

"ORPHEUS WITH HIS LUTE"

Ralph Vaughan Williams, words by William Shakespeare
For Unison Treble Voices and Piano
Oxford University Press Inc. (2007)

CMP Teaching Plan

Analysis

Background Information

Vaughan Williams is considered one of the most important composers of his generation and to be the primary influence in reviving English music in the 20th century. He was born in 1872, the youngest of three children. After his father's death in 1875, his mother moved the family to her childhood home in Surrey. He grew up in an intellectually stimulating family. His maternal aunt taught him piano and violin at a young age. Later education included viola. He attended the Royal College of Music, where he would later teach composition, and Trinity College in Cambridge, eventually earning a degree in music (1894), then history (1895).

As a composer, Vaughan Williams worked to seek the best advice but to use his own judgment. After finishing his degree, he continued at the RCM, studied with Max Bruch in Berlin during his extended honeymoon, and later studied with Maurice Ravel in Paris. He had a close, lifelong friendship with Gustav Holst. Their friendship is notable in that the two composers regularly subjected their work in progress to each other's criticism. During the period "Orpheus with His Lute" was composed, Vaughan Williams was writing primarily vocal music. He was becoming increasingly interested in English folk song and music of the Tudor period.

Vaughan Williams also cared deeply about the longings and struggles of the common people. He never forgot that his music was for people—and was interested in every situation, however humble, for which music was needed. This illumination of the human condition along with his revival of the English musical voice led John F. Kennedy to call him an "extraordinary, ordinary man." His ashes are interred in Westminster Abbey near those of Henry Purcell.

Text

The text comes from Shakespeare's *The Famous History of the Life of King Henry the Eighth.* Queen Katherine, Henry VIII's wife, has been summoned to court to hear the pope's verdict on whether or not Henry may divorce her (in order to marry Anne Boleyn). She pleads with the king, saying she has been a loyal and honest wife for two decades. The king goes over his reasons why his marriage to Katherine is unlawful and must be dissolved. Katherine, furious, refuses to submit to the divorce and sweeps out of court. At the beginning of the next scene, Katherine is in her chambers and says to her serving woman, named Patience, "Take thy lute, wench. My soul grows sad with troubles; Sing and disperse 'em, if thou canst." It is here that "Orpheus" is sung.

Orpheus and Eurydice

Orpheus was the greatest mortal musician, nearly equal to the gods in the excellence of his art. There was no limit to his power when he played the lyre and sang. Both people and nature followed him; trees uprooted themselves, mountains bowed, rivers changed their courses. He fell in love with Eurydice and married her. Immediately after the wedding, as Eurydice was walking in a meadow, a snake bit her and she died. Orpheus's grief was overwhelming; he was determined to go down to the underworld and bring her back. The entire underworld stopped to listen to his music—the Furies and even Hades himself cried and were moved as they listened. Hades allowed Eurydice to travel back with Orpheus, but on one condition: he must not look behind him to see if she followed. Orpheus struggled on the journey but did not look back, until, at the final moment, he couldn't bear it and turned. It was a moment too soon; Eurydice had not yet come into the daylight. She vanished. Orpheus, again overcome with grief, left the company of men and lived in the wilderness, playing for the rocks and rivers and trees. He was eventually killed by a frenzied mob of men who tore his body apart. His head was found by the Muses, who buried it on their sacred island.

Dedication

This piece was dedicated to Lucy Broadwood, active member of the English Folk Song Society, founded in 1989 with the purpose of discovering, collecting, and publishing English folk songs. She was the editor of the society's journal and also a contributor. Other contributors included Vaughan Williams and Percy Grainger.

Sources

The New Grove Dictionary of Music and Musicians, ed. Stanley Sadie, 1980. Macmillan Publishers Limited, "Ralph Vaughan Williams"; "English Folk Dance and Song Society"

Donald J. Grout, *A History of Western Music*, 1973, W. W. Norton & Co.

The Ralph Vaughan Williams Society website: www.rvwsociety.com

The Vaughan Williams Memorial Library, the library and archive of the English Folk Dance and Song Society website: library.efdss.org

Paul Henry Lang, *Music in Western Civilization*, 1997 reprinting, originally 1941, W. W. Norton & Co.

Edith Hamilton, *Mythology*, 1998, 1969, 1942, Little, Brown and Co.

William Shakespeare, edited by S. Schoenbaum, *The Famous History of the Life of King Henry VIII*, 1967. The New American Library.

Musical Analysis

Form

"Orpheus with His Lute" is composed using ternary form, though with slight rhythmic adjustments in the returning "A" idea, altered for the setting of the text. The "A" theme is in F major and the "B" theme is in the relative minor.

Rhythm

The rhythm of the vocal melody is relatively straightforward in order to fulfill its primary objective: text declamation. Half and quarter notes make up the bulk of the melodic line, with occasional dotted quarter-eighth note patterns, used to follow the spoken cadence of a phrase.

Eighth notes are used sparsely in the vocal line but frequently in the piano accompaniment, and then nearly always as passing tones. This rhythmic pulse feels increasingly transfixing as the piece goes on. Significantly, the constant, running eighth note pulse finally slows at m. 25 and then halts in m. 26. It becomes a simple, sustained chord with an augmented, melismatic vocal melody above it, thus illustrating release from care and grief.

Melody

The melodic line is strongly pentatonic. That said, it is also composed nearly entirely from a small, three-note motivic kernel: the interval of a third (either major or minor) followed by a major second. This motif appears first in m. 3 ("lute made trees") but twists up or down over a dozen times in the short—28 measure—melody. This simple three-note motif gets masterful treatment in part because Vaughan Williams, when not using it literally, suggests it, like an aural haunting. Some examples in the way he alters it:

- The interval order of the three notes is inverted so that the second precedes the third (e.g., m. 91, "heads and then")
- Passing tones are used to decorate and fill in the motif. If one mentally removes them and listens only to the rhythmically stressed beats, it's heard yet again. (e.g., m. 7–8 "when he did sing")
- The motif straddles the middle of two distinct phrases. In other words, the first note of the motif is the final note of a phrase, which, to the listener, seems to cut the motif in half (e.g., m. 11–12, "eversprung; as sun" and m. 24, "heart fall")

Looking from a distance, the melody seems to be as familiar and simple as an old English folk song. Looking more closely, it's a dense, intricate, ingenious puzzle—like viewing DNA through a microscope.

Vaughan Williams's choice of these particular three notes is significant, for the motif arises from *do-re* and *sol-mi* patterns from the pentatonic scale. These pitches are the melodic building blocks of the Kodály method (beginning with *sol-mi*, then adding *la*, followed by *re*), which is based on musicological research from a variety of cultures, including English folk songs, and that these patterns of thirds and seconds are the heart of the pentatonic scale. The composer is well known for using pentatonic scales throughout his oeuvre of work, but particularly in this early period of composition. Using the scale as the melodic basis in "Orpheus," Vaughan Williams creates a comfortable, lulling feeling within the listener's subconscious.

Harmony

The piece has a modal flavor, though in F major, and it takes full advantage of the familiar aural relationship between tonic and relative minor. The "home-vacation-back home again" is another way Vaughan Williams creates a piece that seems familiar upon the first listening. The modal color of the harmonies, the way they move and the way they cadence, are familiar and comforting because they are similar to so many folk songs of the British Isles and North America.

Timbre

"Orpheus" is a song of simplicity for voice and piano. The tessitura is from D to D, only an octave, set in the middle of the range in an easy key in which to sing. Therefore, the vocal tone color is not overly bright or dark, just clear and unpretentious, as in a folk song. It's reasonable to expect the musicians to slightly shift the tone color in order to enliven and dramaticize the text. "To his music plants and flowers/Ever sprung, as sun and showers/There had made a lasting spring," necessitates a brighter, lighter sound than "Hung their heads, and then lay by."

Texture

Though only for two instruments, the texture the listener hears is homophonic. In essence, the piano has the same fast-moving harmonic rhythm as the vocal line, supplemented with running eighth notes to add thickness of texture. The piano thus functions as a lute in a 16th-century song. Often in these pieces, the melodic line would be relatively uncomplex, sung in the rhythm of text declamation; the lute would be playing quick, running lines underneath.

On the final phrase, however, the texture thins as this eighth-note pulse slows, then stops. The long, sustained chords are held in the piano. But as the percussive tone dies away, the singer's texture is heard almost alone during the line "fall asleep, or, hearing, die."

Expression

Phrase length generally follows the lines of text. Occasionally, they are slightly altered from the Shakespeare line breaks in order to group related ideas into more modern language conventions and to allow for longer melodic lines. Andante tranquillo (a tranquil walking pace), the tempo marking, is suggested by the context of the poem within Henry VIII. Queen Katherine is in her private rooms, having just come from court where a cardinal from Rome read the pope's decree that the king may divorce her. She pleaded with the king; he was unmoved. She commands her serving woman, Patience, to sing and disperse her troubles. "Orpheus with his Lute" is the result.

The expressive markings used, such as dolce (sweetly), smorzando (extinguished; perform with the sound dying away), decrescendos, piano, the fermata, and the like are used to aid in musical expression of the text. An important moment, however, is the mezzo-forte—the loudest dynamic marking in the piece—a tempo following the smorzando. Thus far in the text we've been hearing about the story of Orpheus; now comes the moral, the reason to be paying attention.

The Heart

The heart of "Orpheus with His Lute" is the magical, lulling power to transfix. The modal flavor, the unflagging use of the pentatonic melodic motif, and the gentle eighth-note rhythm combine to create a hypnotic quieting that reverberates throughout body and soul.

Introducing the Piece

Students read the poem apart from the music and reach understanding of the text by grouping "sentences" together and finding the noun-verb component of each "sentence." Next, review the story of Orpheus and Eurydice. Shakespeare knew the story of Orpheus and used it in his plays. 400 years later, an English composer named Ralph Vaughan Williams, who happened to be quite interested in English music of Shakespeare's time, set the poem to music.

Skill Outcome

Students will perform with a unified sound: matching vowels, balanced dynamics, and accurate intonation.

1. Thinking about unison. Discuss the following: What's the definition of unison? (one sound); Describe a quality unison sound; How does a choir achieve a quality unison sound? Have students brainstorm alone, then pair-share, then create a list on the board. Group like ideas together; connect to the outcome.
2. "The Water Is Wide"—Part 1. Sing the folk song by rote as a warm-up. Work for unified tone, highlighting tall vowels. Use the song in conjunction with other strategies below, such as the listening circles.
3. Matching vowels. Have students mirror each other—facing each other or in small groups. Use hands on the face and other physical gestures to unify placement. Have a few students sing in front of the choir while the choir listens, giving direction on unity vowel shape, then ask one student to sing the "old way" while the rest do it the "new way."
4. Balanced dynamics. Have students sing with eyes down while conductorless to feel as a community. Draw attention to the *mf* at the *a tempo*; discuss why it might be there. Start a singer on a pitch with an "oo" vowel; one by one have others join in to come in without being noticed; then begin *tutti* while the same sound is in the choir's ears; finish by having changed voices drop the octave to be in their tessitura.
5. Listening circles. Form a large circle or concentric circles (depending on room and group size). Singing into the circle helps to hear others; singing with your back to the circle helps more concentrated listening. Employ singers to act as listeners for selected excerpts, and the listeners evaluate the choir's performance.

Assessment

1. Creation of the unison list
2. Teacher observation
3. Self-assessment (mirror activity)
4. Verbal and written feedback when acting as a listener

Knowledge Outcome

Students will identify motifs and evaluate their significance.

1. What's a motif? Ask students, "What words can you think of that begin with "mot"? Share the etymology of the word, connecting the definition of a musical motif to words like motor, motto, mother, or a criminal motif.
2. Discovering motifs in Orpheus. Have students discuss, in a before/after journal assignment, the ways in which their understanding of motif (as employed in Orpheus and elsewhere) will make a difference as they sing the piece. Record "before" ideas; perform without stopping; record "after" observations.
3. Motif scavenger hunt on the iPod. Have students see how many songs they listen to that use motifs. Select questions for discussion: How long is a motif? When is a musical idea too long to classify as a motif? Can a drumbeat pattern be a motif? Do you think this will change how you listen to the songs in which you found the motifs? How? Has it changed how you listen to new music?

Assessment

1. Journal entries
2. Homework scavenger hunt—examples students found

Affective Outcome

Students will explore the powerful symbiotic connection between one's musical choices and their emotions and experiences.

1. The story of Orpheus. Analyze the text of the piece; have students group like ideas together, then find the noun-verb of each. View a slideshow of the story with follow-up discussion and journal question: What do you think Orpheus's music sounded like in order to be powerful enough to bring iron tears down Hades's face, or make a tree uproot?

2. Being a musical detective. Ask students why a particular teacher might play certain music (provide several examples of teachers the students would know). What examples can students recall, to begin to discover the music–emotion connection in the shared school community or in their own lives. Have students speculate on why people choose what they do.

3. Musical symbiosis (to follow Musical Detective). Introduce the term *symbiosis*. On one side of the equation there is the music, and on the other side is the student: How do we choose music that is meaningful to us? Have students discuss matters of musical preference—is it something in the music, in the notes, or is it something in us?

4. Remembering affective experiences. The teacher shares an affective memory related to a musical performance. Ask students to journal, remembering a time when a particular song made a profound emotional impact. What was the song? Where were you? Was it live music or recorded? Was there something important going on in your life? What was the emotion you felt? Tell the story . . .

5. For homework, ask students to interview three close friends, family members, or teachers (must be at least two different generations) about a powerful memory they have around a song. Have students discuss within the choir about surprises they found, or realizations they had. Finally, summarize the ways these stories are connected to the person's emotions and experiences.

6. Performance of Orpheus. Remind students that all the things they have done thus far about emotion in music have to do with being the audience member or the composer. Have them think about the third and final part of the musical triangle—the performer. Ask them how, as performers, they can share their knowledge and feeling about this piece? How can the environment they create make an impression on the audience's emotions and experiences? (Record on video camera and watch.)

Assessment

1. Journal entries
2. Discussion
3. Video recording

Music Selection

Vaughan Williams is considered to be one of the most important composers of English music in the 20th century. This is a masterful piece that is accessible to middle school choirs. It has multiple tie-ins with curriculum topics the students are learning about (pentatonic scales, Orpheus, Shakespeare, for example) and provides an organic, non-cliché way of getting young teenagers to think about why they like the music they like. Reflection on such a charged topic is an important step of broadening one's worldview and being open to new experiences.

NOTE

1. Miriam Altman knew from the beginning of her career that her passion lay in working with young adolescents at the middle school level. She currently teaches chorus and world drumming in grades 5–8 at University School of Milwaukee. An enthusiastic advocate for a richer learning experience in the music classroom, she has been involved with CMP since 1999.

Appendix E

CMP Teaching Plan, "Jody"

Laura K. Sindberg

"JODY"

Timothy Broege
Manhattan Beach Music, 1998

CMP Teaching Plan

Background Information

Born November 6, 1947, and raised in Belmar, New Jersey, the composer Timothy Broege studied piano and theory with Helen Antonides during his childhood years. At Northwestern University he studied composition, receiving the degree bachelor of music with highest honors in 1969.

From 1969 to 1971 the composer taught in the Chicago public school system, after which he served as an elementary school music teacher in Manasquan, New Jersey, until 1980. He currently holds the positions of organist and director of music at First Presbyterian Church in Belmar, a position he has held since 1972, and organist and director of music at the historic Elberon Memorial Church in Elberon, New Jersey.

The music of Timothy Broege has been performed throughout the world by, among others, the Monmouth Symphony Orchestra, the Garden State Philharmonic Orchestra, the Meadows Wind Ensemble, the U.S. Military Academy Band, the New Jersey Chamber Singers, the Atlantic String Quartet, the Cygnus Ensemble, pianist Robert Pollock, guitarist Francis Perry, and recorder virtuoso Jody Miller. He has received numerous grants and commissions from schools, universities, professional performers, and Meet the Composer.

Broege's works include the twenty-one Sinfonias for large ensembles, the series of Songs Without Words for chamber ensembles, and a series of Fantasias for solo instruments, as well as music for voices, keyboards, guitar, recorders, and school bands. His music has been featured at the Boston Early Music Festival, the Midwest Band and Orchestra Clinic, and the College Band Directors National Association.

"Jody" is based on a work song, eight bars long, in a minor pentatonic scale. After the theme is presented in a call-and-response style, the countermelody is introduced. The theme and countermelody go through eight variations, each eight measures in length. Broege states: "Although the structural procedures employed throughout the work are abstract in nature, they do serve a clear narrative scenario in "Jody." As in much programmatic music, the details of the story line are best left to the hearer. Suffice it to say that this is not a happy piece of music: the abuses of brutal penal systems, as well as unjust economic systems, are too much in evidence in the world" (Broege, 1999).

Analysis

Elements of Music

Form

Theme (m. 1–8). After a two-measure introduction, the theme is presented in unison; call-and-response style.

Variation 1 (m. 11–18). Countermelody is introduced—this will remain equally important as the theme throughout the work.

Variation 2 (m. 19–26). Theme in canon; countermelody in low voices.

Variation 3 (m. 27–34). Theme in diminution, call and response between upper woodwinds/xylophone and muted trumpet.

Variation 4 (m. 35–42). Countermelody becomes most prominent, treated in a chorale style. Theme in rhythmic diminution.

Variation 5 (m. 43–50). Tonal center moves to a minor, countermelody is inverted, and theme is presented in rhythmic augmentation. In m. 47–50 the countermelody is inverted and becomes a contrapuntal device.

Variation 6 (m. 51–58). Final melodic gesture of the theme is the basis of this variation, called a "ray of sunshine" by the composer. Percussion very prominent. Tonal center begins to shift downward in m. 55.

Variation 7 (m. 59–65). Tonal center continues to shift; rhythmic placement of the theme also shifts, rhythmic activity and percussion activity increases.

Variation 8 (m. 66–90). Return to original key of c minor, climax of the piece. Entire ensemble is playing: theme in original state in upper voices, countermelody in lower voices. M. 84 is the dynamic high point of "Jody." Augmented note values and gradually softer dynamics serve to conclude the work softly.

Melody

"Jody" is based on a prison work song found in *Wake Up Dead Man: Afro-American Worksongs from Texas Prisons* (Jackson, 1972). It is a minor pentatonic melody, eight bars in length. Throughout "Jody," the melody is manipulated through various compositional devices (see Form) before it returns in its original form at the final variation.

Harmony

"Jody" begins in c minor, where it remains until Variation 5, where it moves to a minor. The tonal center shifts downward in Variations 5, 6, and 7, moving to e, d, and g before returning to c minor for the final variation. Broege employs pedal tones to emphasize c minor. Compositional devices such as fragmentation, augmentation, diminution, and imitation are used to sustain harmonic interest.

Rhythm

The rhythmic and technical requirements of "Jody" are well within capabilities of players in their third year. Rhythmic interest is derived from augmentation and diminution of the countermelody and melody as well as use of percussion instruments, which is extensive.

Timbre

"Jody" begins with two bars of heavy pounding, presented in the percussion section. The use of percussion instruments in "Jody" includes several untuned instruments as well as xylophone and bells, resulting in rich tonal colors. Instrument combinations go well beyond woodwind and brass. Solos for alto saxophone and trumpet.

Texture

Textural variety is provided in each variation through use of compositional devices including fragmentation, diminution, and augmentation (see Form).

Expression

"Jody" is a highly expressive composition, from the sustained notes of the first statement of the theme to the muted conclusion. Interestingly, the piece begins with one beat of silence. Throughout the variations, Broege employs a range of dynamics from pianissimo to fortissimo. While the overall effect of the work is heavy and somber, Variation 6 (m. 51–58) is described as a "ray of sunshine" by the composer.

The Heart of "Jody"

The heart of "Jody" is tragedy. This is a heavy and somber composition, born of one people's oppression over another's.

In his guidelines for performance, Broege emphasizes the somber nature of this composition and its potential for deep lessons for younger musicians: "Less experienced players should be encouraged to leave behind their expressive inhibitions and enter wholeheartedly into the spirit of the piece. The world of "Jody" does not consist of sweetness, triviality, and consumerism. With considerable assistance from the performers, this music has a chance of bearing witness to some of the bad things which a just society may eventually overcome" (Broege, 1998). "Jody" carries rich potential as a vehicle for encouraging students to reflect on their beliefs and values.

Music Selection

- "Jody" is derived from unusual material in comparison to more typical school band works. It is based on a prison work song and employs a minor pentatonic melody.
- This composition provides an opportunity to study a work that is serious in nature, providing an opportunity to discuss social implications of related issues: slavery, punishment, and oppression.
- "Jody" makes interesting use of percussion instruments—these instruments are critical in expressing the programmatic connections of "Jody."
- "Jody" is theme and variations and will help students understand compositional devices such as inversion, repetition, augmentation, and diminution.

Outcomes and Strategies

The students will perform with good phrasing and breathing.

- Warm up with long tones, in c minor concert, reminding students to "breathe big."
- Hum the theme and the countermelody, in four-bar phrases.
- While rehearsing the theme throughout "Jody," remind students to shape phrases with direction and forward motion.
- Record sections of "Jody" and have students evaluate their phrasing, improving as needed.

The students will identify characteristics and name facts about work songs and create a work that represents an aspect of or connection to African-American traditional music.

- Provide students with a brief introduction to the origins of "Jody."
- Have students find related information, through exploring some introductory questions:
  ◦ What are work songs?
  ◦ What are spirituals? Where did they come from?
  ◦ What are the performance traditions for this music? Why did this music exist—what was its purpose?
  ◦ What kind of music exists today that is similar to work songs? Spirituals?

- Using the Jody Connections handout, have students create a representation of a selected aspect of "Jody." Share the works both in class and with the concert audience.
- Discuss contemporary connections: blues, etc. What music would today fit the role of work songs? (e.g., country and western)
- Have students compose a melody in a minor pentatonic scale and add a text in blues style (three repeated phrases and a fourth new phrase).

The students will describe what in the music evokes emotions and explore how the composer evokes meaning in "Jody."

- Discuss some of the distinct ways Broege describes aspects of "Jody" and describe how he evokes meaning through the music.
  - Is "Jody" abstract or programmatic? Describe.
  - Variation 6 is illuminated by a "ray of sunshine." How does Broege evoke this, and why?
  - What is the meaning of m. 84 to the end?
- Have students name songs they are familiar with that evoke a feelingful response and examine what in the music causes those particular kinds of responses.

The students will analyze theme and variation form by describing and labeling its parts and create their own theme and variations.

- Warm up by echoing patterns using three notes of the minor pentatonic scale: 1, ♭3, ♭7. Teacher leads, students lead. Add all notes of the minor pentatonic scale: 1, ♭3, 4, 5, ♭7 and play the theme by ear.
- As students become familiar with the theme and countermelody, have them identify each as they rehearse "Jody" (some devices will be easier to identify than others).
- Label ways in which the melody is changed (on parts).
- Have students create a diagram or graphic representation of "Jody," indicating the theme and each verse.
- Using the minor pentatonic scale on which "Jody" is based, have students compose melodies and later create their own "work song."
- Working in pairs of small groups, students exchange themes and create variations, using techniques employed by Broege.

Assessment

Assessment of the teaching/learning experience of "Jody" will take the form of several tasks, listed under strategies and also listed below.

- Phrasing—Ensemble rehearsal critique.
- Historical/cultural context—"Jody" Connections assignment.
- Analyze form—Have students draw a picture of the form of the piece.
- Connecting to the composer's work, examining his intent (meaning, emotion, and affect)—Student discussions and reflection.

Appendix F

CMP Teaching Plan, "Rhosymedre"

Gary Wolfman

"RHOSYMEDRE" (PRELUDE ON A WELSH HYMN TUNE)

Ralph Vaughan Williams, arr. Wagner
2009 Alfred Music Publishing

CMP Teaching Plan

Music Selection

- "Rhosymedre" has a beautiful melody and countermelody that is aesthetically pleasing to performers and listeners.
- This piece serves as an introduction to the turn-of-the-century English music of Vaughan Williams, Holst, Delius, and Elgar.
- This piece is technically appropriate for all students in the ensemble.
- "Rhosymedre" presents varied examples of orchestration and timbre changes around a given theme, in this case the Welsh hymn tune.

Analysis

- The form of the piece is Introduction-A-A-Extension-Coda (same as introduction).
- The piece is based on a Welsh hymn tune by J. D. Edwards.
- Written in G major, 4/2 throughout.
- All parts have flowing lines surrounding the hymn tune or theme.
- The melody is first presented in the violas and then repeated in octaves by the violins.
- The extension consists of five measures added to the theme the second time it is presented. This is the high point of the piece.

Outcomes, followed by teaching Strategies

- The students will recognize the hymn tune and all countermelodies and be able to perform the themes.
  - Have students learn the theme first by ear through singing and playing, then have them notate the theme on score paper.
  - Have students identify who has the melody and countermelodies and then play dynamics accordingly.
- The students will recognize the form of the piece.
  - Distribute scores to the students (or score excerpts) and have them locate the theme and countermelodies.
  - Through questioning, have students write down in their portfolios what they think the form of "Rhosymedre" is, then write it on the board as a class.
  - Rehearse the piece by form, not by number, letter, or measure number.

- The students will identify the orchestration changes and timbre differences that sustain interest.
  - Ask students to compare how Vaughan Williams changed the setting of the hymn tune in each of the statements or verses.
  - Using the elements of music, have the students write in their portfolios a description of this piece after listening to a professional recording.
  - Listen to selections (one per week, for example) by Holst, Elgar, Delius, and Vaughan Williams and have students write down their impressions of the music and how the composers are similar and different.
  - Have students improvise their own harmony and countermelodies to the hymn tune.
  - Have students play the hymn tune as found in a hymnal setting with the first violins on the soprano line, second violins and violas on the alto line, cellos on the tenor line, and string basses on the bass line; compare and contrast the differences between the hymnal version and Vaughan Williams's.
- The students will perform the piece at a high musical level.

Assessment

- When taking out the piece for rehearsal, ask the students to take out the piece in various ways: in 4/2 time; that does not modulate; whose introduction matches the coda; where the violas have the theme; with the five-measure extension; which has the same rhythm as written on the board.
- Have students play in quartets or double quartets in class. This allows for assessment of progress, builds listening skills, and works toward more musical independence.
- Check dictation and written comments in student portfolios.
- Ask students to contribute their ideas for improving the performance of "Rhosymedre."
- Record the piece in rehearsal and have students write down their impressions—discuss as a class.

Appendix G

CMP Original Proposal[1]: Comprehensive Musicianship through Performance

The attached materials are in support of a proposal for a three-year "comprehensive musicianship" project which I am presenting as a cooperative project of the Wisconsin Music Educators Conference, the Wisconsin School Music Association, and the Wisconsin Department of Public Instruction. The primary purposes of the project include the following:

- To draw attention on a statewide level to the need and potential for developing comprehensive musicianship through performance in our school music programs.
- To provide teachers with guidelines for the development of instructional programs at the local level.
- To provide teachers and administrators with information concerning exemplary programs of "comprehensive musicianship through performance" in Wisconsin schools.
- To involve the Wisconsin Music Educators Conference, the Wisconsin School Music Association, and the Wisconsin Department of Public Instruction in a cooperative project of music education leadership.

COMPREHENSIVE MUSICIANSHIP: RATIONALE

For the purposes of this proposal, "comprehensive musicianship" is defined as a program of instruction which emphasizes the interdependence of musical knowledge and musical performance. It is a program of instruction which seeks, through performance, to develop an understanding of basic musical concepts such as tone, melody, rhythm, harmony, texture, tonality, and form by involving students in a variety of roles including performing, improvising, composing, transcribing, arranging, conducting, rehearsing, and analyzing (visually and aurally).

In spite of philosophical statements by music educators that "general music" is the core of the school music program, the fact is that throughout our state, performing groups at all levels continue to be the foundation of the music program. The quality of performance, community support, school district support, and student involvement in musical performance groups is at its highest level ever in Wisconsin in my opinion. At the same time, the variety of musical performance groups and opportunities has also increased.

Research into performing group curricula and instructional procedures makes it quite clear that the development of performance skills and the actual performance of music do not necessarily lead to meaningful understanding of the concepts mentioned above. While the quality of musical literature has an important effect on the aesthetic responses experienced by students, "high quality" musical literature does not guarantee a higher level of musical understanding. Quoting from a research study done by Charles H. Benner in 1972:

> It can be concluded that performing group participation has little effect on musical behavior other than the acquisition of performance skills unless there is a planned effort by the teacher to enrich the performing experience with additional kinds of musical understanding.

My examination of dozens of music curricula from schools throughout Wisconsin during the last three years leads me to conclude that there is a minimum of "planned effort by the teacher to enrich the performing experience with additional kinds of musical understanding" (Benner, 1972). Or at least if there is such an effort, music educators in Wisconsin are unable to describe it in writing (or verbally) to other people in their school district.

It is important for the further development of music education in Wisconsin that statewide leadership be provided to assist music educators in professional growth and program changes which will move toward the kind of music program which indeed develops "comprehensive musicianship."

COMPREHENSIVE MUSICIANSHIP THROUGH PERFORMANCE

Implications for Curriculum and Instruction

I. Curriculum Philosophy
   a. Music performance is viewed in the context of aesthetic education where music study has value in and for itself.
   b. In performing groups, emphasis is placed on developing "in-depth" experiences through the performance and study of music.
   c. The band and choral curriculum is planned, organized, implemented, and evaluated on the basis of clearly stated objectives for the program and instruction.
   d. Rehearsals become laboratory experiences in musical performance and understanding.
   e. Musical independence as a performer and listener is an important goal of the program.
   f. Instruction utilizes a variety of educational strategies and environments.
II. Possible Teaching/Learning Strategies
   a. Listening and reading assignments
   b. Projects emphasizing creativity
   c. Conducting experiences (leadership roles)
   d. Group discussions, demonstrations, and short lectures
   e. Chamber music study and performance
   f. Field trips
   g. Guest musicians
   h. Workshops, clinics, and festivals
III. Choosing music and other materials

PROJECT ACTIVITIES

Year One

I. Establish a steering committee of one representative from each of the sponsoring agencies (DPI music supervisor, WMEC president-elect, and WSMA executive secretary).
   Responsibilities: (August–December 1977)
   a. Develop specific details of project
   b. Develop criteria for selection of schools and teachers to participate
   c. Promote attendance at comprehensive musicianship sessions at state convention
   d. Identify means of recruiting local teachers for involvement in project
   e. Plan summer workshop format
   f. Hire outside consultant for summer workshop
II. Select and involve 6–8 teachers from local school districts to participate in project as possible model programs.
   Responsibilities: (January–July, 1978) (with steering committee)
   a. Develop format for instruction at local level including instructional objectives, instructional resources, instructional procedures, and evaluation process (primarily during summer workshop)
   b. Plan details of five-day summer workshop
   c. Plan orientation meetings to enlist support and understanding of local school boards and administrators

Year Two

a. Selected educators implement instructional program in their schools.
b. Steering committee monitors progress of local programs.
c. Steering committee plans for evaluation of local programs.
d. Steering committee recruits and selects additional schools and teachers for involvement in the project representing areas of levels of performance not yet involved.
e. Steering committee and teachers develop sessions for state music conference.
f. Steering committee and teachers provide orientation of new school staff.
g. Develop instructional format and plan for teachers new to project.

NOTE

1. Although the original author is not included in this document, it was written by Michael G. George.

Bibliography

Abeles, H. F., Hoffer, R., & Klotman, R. H. (1984, 1995). *Foundations of music education.* New York: Schirmer Books.

Alden, W. L. (1882). Sailor songs. *Harper's New Monthly Magazine, 65,* 283.

Barrett, J. R. (2005). Planning for understanding: A reconceptualized view of the music curriculum. *Music Educators Journal, 91*(4), 17-20.

Benner, C. H. (1972). *Teaching performing groups.* Washington, DC: MENC: The National Association for Music Education.

Biber, H., arranged by Blahnik (1999). *Battalia,* for String Orchestra. Sinsinawa, WI: Alliance Publications Incorporated.

Boyle, J. D. & Radocy, R. E. (1973). Evaluation of instructional objectives in comprehensive musicianship. *Bulletin of the Council for Research in Music Education, 32,* 2-21.

Broege, T. (1999). *Jody,* for Concert Band. Brooklyn, NY: Manhattan Beach Music.

Bruner, J. S. (1977). *The process of education.* Cambridge, MA: Harvard University Press.

Burris, D. L. (1988). *A systematic and integrated approach to teaching comprehensive musicianship and voice in high school performance oriented choirs.* Unpublished doctoral dissertation, Southern Illinois University, Carbondale.

Choksy, L., Abramson, R. M., Gillespie, A. E., Woods, D., & York, F. (2001). *Teaching music in the twenty-first century* (2nd ed.). Englewood Cliffs, NJ: Prentice Hall.

Clandinin, D. J. & Connelly, F. M. (2000). *Narrative inquiry.* San Francisco, CA: Jossey-Bass.

CMP in perspective. (1973). *Music Educators Journal, 59*(9), 34.

Colwell, R. J. & Hewitt, M. (2011). *Teaching of instrumental music* (4th ed.). Upper Saddle River, NJ: Pearson Education, Inc.

Connelly, F. M. & Clandinin, D. J. (1988). *Teachers as curriculum planners: Narratives of experience.* New York: Teachers College Press.

Cooper, L. G. (2004). *Teaching band and orchestra: Methods and materials.* Chicago: GIA Publications.

Consortium of National Arts Education Associations (1994). *The National Standards for Arts Education* Reston, VA: MENC.

Cox, J. (1989). Rehearsal organizational structures used by successful high school choral directors. *Journal of Research in Music Education, 37*(201-218).

Demorest, S. (1996). Structuring a musical choral rehearsal. *Music Educators Journal, 82*(4), 25-30.

Dodson, T. (1989). Are students learning music in band? *Music Educators Journal, 76*(3), 25-29.

Erb, J. (1975). "Shenandoah," SSAATTBB a cappella. Van Nuys, CA: Alfred Publishing Co., Inc.

Farrell, S. (2000). *Tools for powerful student evaluation.* Ft. Lauderdale, FL: Meredith Music.

Gardner, H. (2011). *The unschooled mind* (2nd ed.). New York: Basic Books.

Garofalo, R. & Whaley, G. (1979). Comparison of the unit study and traditional approaches for teaching music through school band performance. *Journal of Research in Music Education, 27*(3), 137-142.

Garofalo, R. (1983). *Blueprint for band.* Ft. Lauderdale, FL: Meredith Music Publications.

Gillespie, R. (2000). Making the school orchestra a treasure. In B. Reimer (Ed.), *Performing with understanding: The challenge of the national standards for music education.* Reston, VA: MENC.

Grainger, P. (1918). *Irish tune from County Derry.* New York: Carl Fischer.

Greene, M. (1984). How do we think about our craft? *Teachers College Record, 86*(1), 55-67.

Grossman, P. (1990). *The making of a teacher.* New York: Teachers College Press.

Gudmundsdottir, S. (1991). Pedagogical models of subject matter. In J. Brophy (Ed.), *Advances in research on teaching* (pp. 265-304). Greenwich, CT: JAI Press.

Heisinger, B. (1991). *Comprehensive musicianship in band instruction.* San Jose State University, San Jose, CA.

Higdon, J. (1999). *A quiet moment.* Philadelphia, PA: Lawdon Press.

Hylton, J. B. (1995). *Comprehensive choral music education.* Upper Saddle River, NJ: Prentice Hall.

Keene, J. A. (1987). *A history of music education in the United States* (2nd ed.). Hanover: University Press of New England.

Kennell, R. (2002). Musical thinking in the instrumental rehearsal. In E. Boardman (Ed.), *Dimensions of musical learning and teaching*. Reston, VA: MENC.

Kinyon, J. (1990). *Londonderry air*. Van Nuys, CA: Alfred Music Publishing.

Kohut, D. L. (1996). *Instrumental music pedagogy*. Champaign, IL: Stipes Publishing.

Labuta, J. A. (1997). *Teaching musicianship in the high school band*. Ft. Lauderdale, FL: Meredith Music Publications.

Larsen, C. (2000). Interview with Larry Rachleff. In B. Reimer (Ed.), *Performing with understanding: The challenge of the national standards for music education*. Reston, VA: MENC.

Leglar, M. & Collay, M. (2002). Research by teachers on teacher education. In R. Colwell & C. P. Richardson (Eds.), *The new handbook of research on music teaching and learning* (pp. 855–73). New York: Oxford University Press.

Lehman, P. R. (1986). Teaching music in the 1990's. *Dialogue in Instrumental Music Education, 10*(1), 3–18.

Lehman, P. R. (1999). How can the skills and knowledge called for in the national standards best be taught? In *Vision 2020: The Housewright symposium on the future of music education*. Reston, VA: MENC.

Lehman, P. R. (2000). The power of the national standards for music education. In B. Reimer (Ed.), *Performing with understanding: The challenge of the national standards for music education*. Reston, VA: MENC.

Leonhard, C. & House, R. W. (1972). *Foundations and principles of music education*. New York: McGraw-Hill Inc.

Library of Congress (n. d.), Song of America Project. Downloaded from http://www.loc.gov/creativity/hampson/ Washington, DC: Author.

Lomax, A. (1975). *The folk songs of North America*. New York: Dolphin Books, Doubleday & Company.

Lomax, J. A. & Lomax, A. (1994). *American ballads and folk songs*. New York: Dover Publications.

Mark, M. L. (1996). *Contemporary music education* (3rd ed.). New York: Schirmer Books.

Mark, M. L. (2000). From Tanglewood to Tallahassee in 32 years. *Music Educators Journal, 86*(5), 25–28.

Mitchell, W. J. (1969). Under the comprehensive musicianship umbrella. *Music Educators Journal, 55*(7), 71–75.

Music Educators National Conference (1994). *Teaching examples: Ideas for music educators*. Reston, VA: Author. (No longer available.)

Music Educators National Conference. (1996). *Performance standards for music: Strategies and benchmarks for assessing progress toward the national standards, grades preK-12*. Reston, VA: Author.

Odegaard, D. (2009). *Music curriculum writing 101*. Chicago: GIA Publications.

O'Toole, P. A. (2003). *Shaping sound musicians*. Chicago: GIA Publications.

Pink, D. H. (2006). *A whole new mind*. New York: Riverhead Books.

Pontious, M. (2002). Taking the longer view. *The Wisconsin School Musician*, Volume 72, No. 3, 12.

Raph, Theodore. (1964). *The American song treasury*. Mineola, NY: Dover Publications.

Ravitch, D. (2010). *The death and life of the great American school system*. New York: Basic Books.

Reimer, B. (2000). What is "performing with understanding?" In B. Reimer (Ed.), *Performing with understanding: The challenge of the national standards for music education* (pp. 11-29). Reston, VA: MENC.

Reimer, B. (2003). *A philosophy of music education: Advancing the vision*. Upper Saddle River, NJ: Prentice Hall.

Reynolds, R. (2000). Repertoire is the curriculum. *Music Educators Journal, 87*(1), 31–33.

Santelli, R. & George-Warren, H. (2001). *American roots music*. New York: Abrams Books.

Schmidt, M. (1998). Defining "good" music teaching: Four student teachers' beliefs and practices. *Bulletin of the Council for Research in Music Education, 138*, 19–46.

Shank, J. (2005). *Musica animam tangens*. Santa Barbara, CA: Santa Barbara Music Publishing.

Sherburn, E. F. (1984). *Student achievement and attitude in high school instrumental music education: A comparison of the effects of a lab approach and a more traditional approach*. Unpublished doctoral dissertation, University of Southern California, Los Angeles.

Shulman, L. S. (1986). Those who understand: Knowledge growth in teaching. *Educational Researcher, 15*(2), 4–14.

Shulman, L. S. (1987). Knowledge and teaching: Foundations of the new reform. *Harvard Educational Review, 57*(1), 1–22.

Sindberg, L. K. (1998). Concerts that teach. *Teaching Music, 5*(6), 36–37.

Sindberg, L. K. (2006). *Comprehensive musicianship through performance (CMP) in the lived experience of students*. Unpublished doctoral dissertation, Northwestern University, Evanston, IL.

Sindberg, L. K. (2009). The evolution of comprehensive musicianship through performance (CMP)—A model for teaching performing with understanding in the ensemble setting. *Contributions to Music Education, 36*(1), 25–39.

Snow, S. & Apfelstadt, H. (2002). Musical thinking and learning in the choral context. In E. Boardman (Ed.), *Dimensions of musical learning and teaching: A different kind of classroom*. Reston, VA: MENC.

Sousa, J. P. (1897). *The stars and stripes forever*. New York: The John Church Company. Downloaded from www.mutopiaproject.org.

Spradling, R. L. (1985). The effect of timeout from performance on attentiveness and attitude of university band students. *Journal of Research in Music Education, 33*(2), 123–37.

Stamp, J. (1996). *Ere the world began to be*. New Glarus, WI: Daehn Publications.

Swearingen, K. D. (1993). *A study of the effectiveness of the inclusion of a music appreciation learning module as a supplement to the traditional high school band performance curriculum*. Unpublished doctoral dissertation, University of Southern California, Los Angeles.

Thomas, R. (1970). *Manhattanville music curriculum program*. Final report (Report No. BR 6-1999). Purchase, NY: Manhattanville College.

Thomson, W. (1970). Music rides a wave of reform in Hawaii. *Music Educators Journal, 56*(9), 72–76.

Ticheli, F. (1999). "Shenandoah." Brooklyn, NY: Manhattan Beach Music.

Ticheli, F. (2004). *A Shaker gift song*. Brooklyn, NY: Manhattan Beach Music.

Tunks, T. (1992). The transfer of music learning. In R. Colwell (Ed.), *The handbook of research on music teaching and learning* (pp. 437–47). New York: Schirmer Books.

Wersen, L. G. (1968). New directions for music education. *Music Educators Journal, 54*(7), 71.

Wiggins, J. (2001). *Teaching for musical understanding*. Boston: McGraw-Hill.

Willoughby, D. (1971). *Comprehensive musicianship and the undergraduate music curricula*. Washington, DC: MENC.

Winner, E., (Ed.). (1995). *Arts PROPEL: An introductory handbook*. Cambridge, MA: Project Zero Publications.

Wisconsin Music Educators Association (WMEA). (1977). *Comprehensive musicianship through performance*. [Brochure] Madison, WI: Author.

Wisconsin Music Educators Association. [Brochure] (est. 1977) *Background of the Wisconsin Comprehensive Musicianship through Performance Project*.

Witt, A. C. (1986). Use of class time and student attentiveness in secondary instrumental music rehearsals. *Journal of Research in Music Education*, 34 (34–42).

Wolf, D. P. (1991). *Taking full measure: Rethinking assessment through the arts*. New York: College Entrance Examination Board.

Woods, G. D. (1972). *Comprehensive musicianship*. Independent School Bulletin, 32(1), 61–63.

Index

About the Author

Laura K. Sindberg is assistant professor of music education at the University of Minnesota, where she teaches undergraduate and graduate courses in music education. Prior to earning her doctorate at Northwestern University, Dr. Sindberg taught public school music for seventeen years, during which time she became heavily involved in Comprehensive Musicianship through Performance—also the topic of her dissertation research. Dr. Sindberg continues to be actively involved with CMP in all facets of her teaching and has written and presented extensively on the topic.

CPSIA information can be obtained at www.ICGtesting.com
Printed in the USA
BVOW051103200312

285581BV00004B/1/P

Made in the USA
Middletown, DE
20 January 2015